Landmarks in French Literature

Landmarks in French Literature

Lytton Strachey

MINT EDITIONS

Landmarks in French Literature was first published in 1912.

This edition published by Mint Editions 2021.

ISBN 9781513278490 | E-ISBN 9781513278957

Published by Mint Editions®

MINT
EDITIONS

minteditionbooks.com

Publishing Director: Jennifer Newens
Design & Production: Rachel Lopez Metzger
Project Manager: Micaela Clark
Typesetting: Westchester Publishing Services

CONTENTS

I

Origins—The Middle Ages

When the French nation gradually came into existence among the ruins of the Roman civilization in Gaul, a new language was at the same time slowly evolved. This language, in spite of the complex influences which went to the making of the nationality of France, was of a simple origin. With a very few exceptions, every word in the French vocabulary comes straight from the Latin. The influence of the pre-Roman Celts is almost imperceptible; while the number of words introduced by the Frankish conquerors amounts to no more than a few hundreds. Thus the French tongue presents a curious contrast to that of England. With us, the Saxon invaders obliterated nearly every trace of the Roman occupation; but though their language triumphed at first, it was eventually affected in the profoundest way by Latin influences; and the result has been that English literature bears in all its phases the imprint of a double origin. French literature, on the other hand, is absolutely homogeneous. How far this is an advantage or the reverse it would be difficult to say; but the important fact for the English reader to notice is that this great difference does exist between the French language and his own. The complex origin of the English tongue has enabled English writers to obtain those effects of diversity, of contrast, of imaginative strangeness, which have played such a dominating part in our literature. The genius of the French language, descended from its single Latin stock, has triumphed most in the contrary direction—in simplicity, in unity, in clarity, and in restraint.

Some of these qualities are already distinctly visible in the earliest French works which have come down to us—the *Chansons de Geste*. These poems consist of several groups or cycles of narrative verse, cast in the epic mould. It is probable that they first came into existence in the eleventh and twelfth centuries; and they continued to be produced in various forms of repetition, rearrangement, and at last degradation, throughout the Middle Ages. Originally they were not written, but recited. Their authors were the wandering minstrels, who found, in the crowds collected together at the great fairs and places of pilgrimage of those early days, an audience for long narratives of romance and adventure drawn from the Latin chronicles and the monkish traditions of a still more remote past. The earliest, the most famous, and the finest of these poems is the *Chanson de Roland*, which recounts the mythical incidents of a battle between Charlemagne, with 'all his peerage', and the hosts of the Saracens. Apart from some touches of the marvellous—such as the two hundred years of Charlemagne and the intervention of angels—the whole atmosphere of the work is that of eleventh-century France, with its aristocratic society, its barbaric vigour, its brutality, and its high sentiments of piety and honour. The beauty of the poem lies in the grand simplicity of its style. Without a trace of the delicacy and variety of a Homer, farther still from the consummate literary power of a Virgil or a Dante, the unknown minstrel who composed the *Chanson de Roland* possessed nevertheless a very real gift of art. He worked on a large scale with a bold confidence. Discarding absolutely the aids of ornament and the rhetorical elaboration of words, he has succeeded in evoking with an extraordinary, naked vividness the scenes of strife and heroism which he describes. At his best—in the lines of farewell between Roland and Oliver, and the well-known account of Roland's death—he rises to a restrained and severe pathos which is truly sublime. This great work—bleak, bare, gaunt, majestic—stands out, to the readers of to-day, like some huge mass of ancient granite on the far horizon of the literature of France.

While the *Chansons de Geste* were developing in numerous cycles of varying merit, another group of narrative poems, created under different influences, came into being. These were the *Romans Bretons*, a series of romances in verse, inspired by the Celtic myths and traditions which still lingered in Brittany and England. The spirit of these poems was very different from that of the *Chansons de Geste*. The latter were the typical offspring of the French genius—positive, definite, materialistic; the former were impregnated with all the dreaminess, the mystery, and the romantic spirituality of the Celt. The legends upon which they were based revolved for the most part round the history of King Arthur and his knights; they told of the strange adventures of Lancelot, of the marvellous quest of the Holy Grail, of the overwhelming and fatal loves of Tristan and Yseult. The stories gained an immense popularity in France, but they did not long retain their original character. In the crucible of the facile and successful CHRÉTIEN DE TROYES, who wrote towards the close of the twelfth century, they assumed a new complexion; their mystical strangeness became transmuted into the more commonplace magic of wizards and conjurers, while their elevated, immaterial conception of love was replaced by the superfine affectations of a mundane gallantry. Nothing shows more clearly at what an early date, and with what strength, the most characteristic qualities of French literature were developed, than the way in which the vague imaginations of the Celtic romances were metamorphosed by French writers into the unambiguous elegances of civilized life.

Both the *Chansons de Geste* and the *Romans Bretons* were aristocratic literature: they were concerned with the life and ideals—the martial prowess, the chivalric devotion, the soaring honour—of the great nobles of the age. But now another form of literature arose which depicted, in short verse narratives, the more ordinary conditions of middle-class life. These *Fabliaux*, as they were called, are on the whole of no great value as works of art; their poetical form is usually poor, and their substance exceedingly gross. Their chief interest lies in the fact that they reveal, no less clearly than the aristocratic *Chansons*, some of the most abiding qualities of the French genius. Its innate love of absolute realism and its peculiar capacity for cutting satire—these characteristics appear in the *Fabliaux* in all their completeness. In one or two of the stories, when the writer possesses a true vein of sensibility and taste, we find a surprising vigour of perception and a remarkable psychological power. Resembling the *Fabliaux* in their realism and their bourgeois outlook, but far more delicate and witty, the group of poems known as the *Roman de Renard* takes a high place in the literature of the age. The humanity, the dramatic skill, and the command of narrative power displayed in some of these pleasant satires, where the foibles and the cunning of men and women are thinly veiled under the disguise of animal life, give a foretaste of the charming art which was to blossom forth so wonderfully four centuries later in the Fables of La Fontaine.

One other work has come down to us from this early epoch, which presents a complete contrast, both with the rough, bold spirit of the *Chansons de Geste* and the literal realism of the *Fabliaux*. This is the 'chante-fable' (or mingled narrative in verse and prose) of *Aucassin et Nicolete*. Here all is delicacy and exquisiteness—the beauty, at once fragile and imperishable, of an enchanting work of art. The unknown author has created, in his light, clear verse and his still more graceful and poetical prose, a delicious atmosphere of delicate romance. It is 'the tender eye-dawn of aurorean love' that he shows us—the happy, sweet, almost childish passion of two young creatures who move, in absolute innocence and beauty, through a wondrous world of their own. The youth Aucassin, who rides into the fight dreaming of his beloved, who sees her shining among the stars in heaven—

> *Estoilette, je te voi,*
> *Que la lune trait à soi;*
> *Nicolete est avec toi,*
> *M'amiete o le blond poil.*

> *(Little star, I see thee there,*
> *That the moon draws close to her!*
> *Nicolette is with thee there,*
> *My love of the yellow hair.)*—

who disdains the joys of Paradise, since they exclude the joys of loving—

En paradis qu'ai-je a faire? Je n'i quier entrer, mais que j'aie Nicolete, ma très douce amie que j'aime tant. . . Mais en enfer voil jou aler. Car en enfer vont li bel clerc et li bel cevalier, qui sont mort as tournois et as rices guerres, et li bien sergant, et li franc homme. . . Avec ciax voil jou aler, mais que j'aie Nicolete, ma très douce amie, avec moi. (What have I to do in Paradise? I seek not to enter there, so that I have Nicolette, my most sweet friend, whom I love so well. . . But to Hell will I go. For to Hell go the fine clerks and the fine knights, who have died in tourneys and in rich wars, and the brave soldiers and the free-born men. . . With these will I go, so that I have Nicolette, my most sweet friend, with me.)

—Aucassin, at once brave and naïf, sensuous and spiritual, is as much the type of the perfect medieval lover as Romeo, with his ardour and his vitality, is of the Renaissance one. But the poem—for in spite of the prose passages, the little work is in effect simply a poem—is not all sentiment and dreams. With admirable art the author has interspersed here and there contrasting episodes of realism or of absurdity; he has woven into his story a succession of vivid dialogues, and by means of an acute sense of observation he has succeeded in keeping his airy fantasy in touch with actual things. The description of Nicolette, escaping from her prison, and stepping out over the grass in her naked feet, with the daisies, as she treads on them, showing black against her whiteness, is a wonderful example of his power of combining imagination with detail, beauty with truth. Together with the *Chanson de Roland*—though in such an infinitely different style—*Aucassin et Nicolete* represents the most valuable elements in the French poetry of this early age.

With the thirteenth century a new development began, and one of the highest importance—the development of Prose. *La Conquête de Constantinople*, by VILLEHARDOUIN, written at the beginning of the century, is the earliest example of those historical memoirs which were afterwards to become so abundant in French literature; and it is written, not in the poetical prose of *Aucassin et Nicolete*, but in the simple, plain style of straightforward narrative. The book cannot be ranked among the masterpieces; but it has the charm of sincerity and that kind of pleasant flavour which belong to innocent antiquity. The good old Villehardouin has something of the engaging *naïveté*, something of the romantic curiosity, of Herodotus. And in spite of the sobriety and dryness of his writing he can, at moments, bring a sense of colour and movement into his words. His description of the great fleet of the crusaders, starting from Corfu, has this fine sentence: 'Et le jour fut clair et beau: et le vent doux et bon. Et ils laissèrent aller les voiles au vent.' His account of the spectacle of Constantinople, when it appeared for the first time to the astonished eyes of the Christian nobles, is well known: 'Ils ne pouvaient croire que si riche ville pût être au monde, quand ils virent ces hauts murs et ces riches tours dont elle était close tout autour à la ronde, et ces riches palais et ces hautes églises. . . Et sachez qu'il n'y eut si hardi à qui la chair ne frémit; et ce ne fut une merveille; car jamais si grande affaire ne fut entreprise de nulles gens, depuis que le monde fut créé.' Who does not feel at such words as these, across the ages, the thrill of the old adventure!

A higher level of interest and significance is reached by JOINVILLE in his *Vie de Saint Louis*, written towards the close of the century. The fascination of the book lies in its human qualities. Joinville narrates, in the easy flowing tone of familiar conversation, his reminiscences of the good king in whose service he had spent the active years of his life, and whose memory he held in adoration. The deeds, the words, the noble sentiments, the saintly devotion of Louis—these things he relates with a charming and ingenuous sympathy, yet with a perfect freedom and an absolute veracity. Nor is it only the character of his master that Joinville has brought into his pages; his book is as much a self-revelation as a biography. Unlike Villehardouin, whose chronicle shows hardly a trace of personal feeling, Joinville speaks of himself unceasingly, and has impressed his work indelibly with the mark of his own individuality. Much of its charm depends upon the contrast which he thus almost unconsciously reveals between himself and his master— the vivacious, common-sense, eminently human nobleman, and the grave, elevated, idealizing king. In their conversations, recounted with such detail and such relish by Joinville, the whole force of this contrast becomes delightfully apparent. One seems to see in them, compressed and symbolized in the characters of these two friends, the conflicting qualities of sense and spirit, of worldliness and self-immolation, of the most shrewd and literal perspicacity and the most visionary exaltation, which make up the singular antithesis of the Middle Ages.

A contrast no less complete, though of a different nature, is to be found in the most important poetical work of the thirteenth century— *Le Roman de la Rose.* The first part of this curious poem was composed by GUILLAUME DE LORRIS, a young scholar who wrote for that aristocratic public which, in the previous generation, had been fascinated by the courtly romances of Chrétien de Troyes. Inspired partly by that writer, and partly by Ovid, it was the aim of Lorris to produce an *Art of Love*, brought up to date, and adapted to the tastes of his aristocratic audience, with all the elaborate paraphernalia of learned disquisition and formal gallantry which was then the mode. The poem, cast in the form of an intricate allegory, is of significance chiefly on account of its immense popularity, and for its being the fountain-head of a school of allegorical poetry which flourished for many centuries in France. Lorris died before he had finished his work, which, however, was destined to be completed in a singular manner. Forty years later, another young scholar, JEAN DE MEUNG, added to the 4000 lines which Lorris had left no fewer than 18,000 of his own. This vast addition was not only quite out of proportion but also quite out of tone with the original work. Jean de Meung abandoned entirely the refined and aristocratic atmosphere of his predecessor, and wrote with all the realism and coarseness of the middle class of that day. Lorris's vapid allegory faded into insignificance, becoming a mere peg for a huge mass of extraordinarily varied discourse. The whole of the scholastic learning of the Middle Ages is poured in a confused stream through this remarkable and deeply interesting work. Nor is it merely as a repository of medieval erudition that Jean de Meung's poem deserves attention; for it is easy to perceive in it an intellectual tendency far in advance of its age—a spirit which, however trammelled by antiquated conventions, yet claims kinship with that of Rabelais, or even that of Voltaire. Jean de Meung was not a great artist; he wrote without distinction, and without sense of form; it is his bold and voluminous thought that gives him a high place in French literature. In virtue alike of his popularization of an encyclopedic store of knowledge and of his underlying doctrine—the worship of Nature—he ranks as a true forerunner of the great movement of the Renaissance.

The intellectual stirring, which seemed to be fore-shadowed by the second part of the *Roman de la Rose*, came to nothing. The disasters and confusion of the Hundred Years War left France with very little energy either for art or speculation; the horrors of a civil war followed; and thus the fourteenth and fifteenth centuries are perhaps the emptiest in the annals of her literature. In the fourteenth century one great writer embodied the character of the time. FROISSART has filled his splendid pages with 'the pomp and circumstance of glorious war'. Though he spent many years and a large part of his fortune in the collection of materials for his history of the wars between France and England, it is not as an historian that he is now remembered; it is as a writer of magnificent prose. His *Chroniques*, devoid of any profundity of insight, any true grasp of the movements of the age, have rarely been paralleled in the brilliance and animation of their descriptions, the vigour of their character-drawing, the flowing picturesqueness of their style. They unroll themselves like some long tapestry, gorgeously inwoven with scenes of adventure and chivalry, with flags and spears and chargers, and the faces of high-born ladies and the mail-clad figures of knights. Admirable in all his descriptions, it is in his battle-pieces that Froissart particularly excels. Then the glow of his hurrying sentences redoubles, and the excitement and the bravery of the combat rush out from his pen in a swift and sparkling stream. One sees the serried ranks and the flashing armour, one hears the clash of weapons and the shouting of the captains: 'Montjoie! Saint Denis! Saint George! Giane!'—one feels the sway and the press and the tumult, one laments with the vanquished, one exults with the victors, and, amid the glittering panoply of 'grand seigneur, conte, baron, chevalier, et escuier', with their high-sounding titles and their gallant prowess, one forgets the reverse side of all this glory—the ravaged fields, the smoking villages, the ruined peasants—the long desolation of France.

The Chronicles of Froissart are history seen through the eyes of a herald; the *Memoirs* of PHILIPPE DE COMMYNES are history envisaged by a politician and a diplomatist. When Commynes wrote—towards the close of the fifteenth century—the confusion and strife which Froissart had chronicled with such a gusto were things of the past, and France was beginning to emerge as a consolidated and centralized state. Commynes himself, one of the confidential ministers of Louis XI, had played an important part in this development; and his book is the record of the triumphant policy of his crafty and sagacious sovereign. It is a fine piece of history, written with lucidity and firmness, by a man who had spent all his life behind the scenes, and who had never been taken in. The penetration and the subtlety of Commynes make his work interesting chiefly for its psychological studies and for the light that it throws on those principles of cunning statecraft which permeated the politics and diplomacy of the age and were to receive their final exposition in the *Prince* of Machiavelli. In his calm, judicious, unaffected pages we can trace the first beginnings of that strange movement which was to convert the old Europe of the Middle Ages, with its universal Empire and its universal Church, into the new Europe of independent secular nations—the Europe of to-day.

Commynes thus stands on the brink of the modern world; though his style is that of his own time, his matter belongs to the future: he looks forward into the Renaissance. At the opposite end of the social scale from this rich and powerful diplomatist, VILLON gave utterance in language of poignant beauty to the deepest sentiments of the age that was passing away. A ruffian, a robber, a murderer, haunting the vile places of Paris, flying from justice, condemned, imprisoned, almost executed, and vanishing at last, none knows how or where, this extraordinary genius lives now as a poet and a dreamer—an artist who could clothe in unforgettable verse the intensest feelings of a soul. The bulk of his work is not large. In his *Grand Testament*—a poem of about 1500 lines, containing a number of interspersed ballades and rondeaus—in his *Petit Testament*, and in a small number of miscellaneous poems, he has said all that he has to say. The most self-communicative of poets, he has impressed his own personality on every line that he wrote. Into the stiff and complicated forms of the rondeau and rondel, the ballade and double ballade, with their limited rhymes and their enforced repetitions, he has succeeded in breathing not only the spirit of beauty, but the spirit of individuality. He was not a simple character; his melancholy was shot with irony and laughter; sensuality and sentimentality both mingled with his finest imaginations and his profoundest visions; and all these qualities are reflected, shifting and iridescent, in the magic web of his verse. One thought, however, perpetually haunts him; under all his music of laughter or of passion, it is easy to hear one dominating note. It is the thought of mortality. The whining, leering, brooding creature can never for a moment forget that awful Shadow. He sees it in all its aspects—as a subject for mockery, for penitence, for resignation, for despair. He sees it as the melancholy, inevitable end of all that is beautiful, all that is lovely on earth.

> *Dictes moi où, n'en quel pays*
> *Est Flora, la belle Rommaine;*
> *Archipiada, ne Thaïs—*

and so through the rest of the splendid catalogue with its sad, unanswerable refrain—

> *Mais où sont les neiges d'antan?*

Even more persistently, the vision rises before him of the physical terrors of death—the hideousness of its approaches, the loathsomeness of its corruptions; in vain he smiles, in vain he weeps; the grim imagination will not leave him. In the midst of his wildest debauches, he suddenly remembers the horrible features of decaying age; he repents; but there, close before him, he sees the fatal gibbet, and his own body swinging among the crows.

With Villon the medieval literature of France comes at once to a climax and a termination. His potent and melancholy voice vibrates with the accumulated passion and striving and pain of those far-off generations, and sinks mysteriously into silence with the birth of a new and happier world.

II

The Renaissance

There is something dark and wintry about the atmosphere of the later Middle Ages. The poems of Villon produce the impression of some bleak, desolate landscape of snow-covered roofs and frozen streets, shut in by mists, and with a menacing shiver in the air. It is—

> *sur la morte saison,*
> *Que les loups se vivent de vent,*
> *Et qu'on se tient en sa maison,*
> *Pour le frimas, près du tison.*

Then all at once the grey gloom lifts, and we are among the colours, the sunshine, and the bursting vitality of spring.

The great intellectual and spiritual change which came over western Europe at the beginning of the sixteenth century was the result of a number of converging causes, of which the most important were the diffusion of classical literature consequent upon the break-up of the Byzantine Empire at the hands of the Turks, the brilliant civilization of the Italian city-states, and the establishment, in France, Spain and England, of powerful monarchies whose existence ensured the maintenance of order and internal peace. Thus it happened that the splendid literature of the Ancient World—so rich in beauty and so significant in thought—came into hands worthy of receiving it. Scholars, artists and thinkers seized upon the wondrous heritage and found in it a whole unimagined universe of instruction and delight. At the same time the physical discoveries of explorers and men of science opened out vast fresh regions of speculation and adventure. Men saw with astonishment the old world of their fathers vanishing away, and, within them and without them, the dawning of a new heaven and a new earth. The effect on literature of these combined forces was enormous. In France particularly, under the strong and brilliant government of Francis I, there was an outburst of original and vital writing. This literature, which begins, in effect, what may be called the distinctively *modern* literature of France, differs in two striking respects from that of the Middle Ages. Both in their attitude towards art and in their attitude towards thought, the great writers of the Renaissance inaugurated a new era in French literature.

The new artistic views of the age first appeared, as was natural, in the domain of poetry. The change was one towards consciousness and deliberate, self-critical effort. The medieval poets had sung with beauty; but that was not enough for the poets of the Renaissance: they determined to sing not only with beauty, but with care. The movement began in the verse of MAROT, whose clear, civilized, worldly poetry shows for the first time that tendency to select and to refine, that love of ease and sincerity, and that endeavour to say nothing that is not said well, which were to become the fundamental characteristics of all that was best in French poetry for the next three hundred years. In such an exquisite little work of art as his epistle in three-syllabled verse—'À une Damoyselle Malade', beginning—

> *Ma mignonne,*
> *Je vous donne*
> *Le bonjour,*

we already have, in all its completeness, that tone of mingled distinction, gaiety and grace which is one of the unique products of the mature poetical genius of France. But Marot's gift was not wide enough for the voluminous energies of the age; and it was not until a generation later, in the work of the *Pléiade*—a group of writers of whom RONSARD was the chief, and who flourished about the middle of the sixteenth century—that the poetical spirit of the French Renaissance found its full expression.

The mere fact that the *Pléiade* formed a definite school, with common principles and a fixed poetical creed, differentiates them in a striking way from the poets who had preceded them. They worked with no casual purpose, no merely professional art, but with a high sense of the glory of their calling and a noble determination to give to the Muses whom they worshipped only of their best. They boldly asserted—in Du Bellay's admirable essay, *La Défense et Illustration de la Langue Française*—the right of the French language to stand beside those of the ancients, as a means of poetical expression; and they devoted their lives to the proof of their doctrine. But their respect for their own tongue by no means implied a neglect of the Classics. On the contrary, they shared to the full the adoration of their contemporaries for the learning and the literature of the Ancient World. They were scholars as well as poets; and their great object was to create a tradition in the poetry of France which should bring it into accord with the immortal models of Greece and Rome. This desire to imitate classical literature led to two results. In the first place, it led to the invention of a great number of new poetical forms, and the abandonment of the old narrow and complicated conventions which had dominated the poetry of the Middle Ages. With the free and ample forms of the Classics before them, Ronsard and his school enfranchised French verse. Their technical ability was very great; and it is hardly too much to say that the result of their efforts was the creation of something hitherto lacking in French literature—a poetical instrument which, in its strength, its freedom, its variety of metrical resources, and its artistic finish, was really adequate to fulfil the highest demands of genius. In this direction their most important single achievement was their elevation of the 'Alexandrine' verse—the great twelve-syllabled rhyming couplet—to that place of undisputed superiority over all other metres which it has ever since held in French poetry.

But the *Pléiade's* respect for classical models led to another and a far less fortunate result. They allowed their erudition to impinge upon their poetry, and, in their eagerness to echo the voice of antiquity, they too often failed to realize the true bent either of their own language or their own powers. This is especially obvious in the longer poems of Ronsard—his *Odes* and his *Françiade*—where all the effort and skill of the poet have not been enough to save his verse from tedium and inflation. The Classics swam into the ken of these early discoverers in such a blaze of glory that their eyes were dazzled and their feet misled. It was owing to their very eagerness to imitate their great models exactly—to 'ape the outward form of majesty'—that they failed to realize the true inward spirit of Classical Art.

It is in their shorter poems—when the stress of classical imitation is forgotten in the ebullition of individual genius—that Ronsard and his followers really come to their own. These beautiful lyrics possess the freshness and charm of some clear April morning, with its delicate flowers and its carolling birds. It is the voice of youth that sings in light and varied measures, composed with such an exquisite happiness, such an unlaboured art. The songs are of Love and of Nature, of roses, skylarks and kisses, of blue skies and natural joys. Sometimes there is a sadder note; and the tender music reminds us of the ending of pleasures and the hurrying steps of Time. But with what a different accent from that of the dark and relentless Villon! These gentle singers had no words for such brutalities.

Quand vous serez bien vieille, au soir, à la chandelle—

so Ronsard addresses his mistress; and the image is a charming one of quiet and refined old age, with its half-smiling memories of vanished loves. What had become, in the hands of Villon, a subject for grim jests and horrible descriptions, gave to Ronsard simply an opportunity for the delicate pathos of regret. Then again the note changes, and the pure, tense passion of Louise Labé—

Oh! si j'étais en ce beau sein ravie
De celui-là pour lequel vais mourant—

falls upon our ears. And then, in the great sonnet sequence of Du Bellay—*Les Antiquités de Rome*—we hear a splendid sound unknown before in French poetry—the sonorous boom of proud and pompous verse.

Contemporary with the poetry of the *Pléiade*, the influence of the Renaissance spirit upon French literature appeared with even more striking force in the prose of RABELAIS. The great achievement of the *Pléiade* had been the establishment, once and for all, of the doctrine that literature was something essentially artistic; it was Rabelais who showed that it possessed another quality—that it was a mighty instrument of thought. The intellectual effort of the Middle Ages had very rarely clothed itself in an artistic literary form. Men laughed or wept in the poetry or prose of their own tongue; but they thought in scholastic Latin. The work of Jean de Meung was an exception; but, even there, the poetical form was rough and feeble; the artistic and the intellectual principles had not coalesced. The union was accomplished by Rabelais. Far outstripping Jean de Meung in the comprehensiveness and vigour of his thought, he at the same time infinitely surpassed him as an artist. At first sight, indeed, his great book hardly conveys such an impression; to a careless reader it might appear to be simply the work of a buffoon or a madman. But such a conception of it would be totally mistaken. The more closely one examines it, the more forcibly one must be struck alike by its immense powers of intellect and its consummate literary ability. The whole vast spirit of the Renaissance is gathered within its pages: the tremendous vitality, the enormous erudition, the dazzling optimism, the courage, the inventiveness, the humanity, of that extraordinary age. And these qualities are conveyed to us, not by some mere conscientious pedant, or some clumsy enthusiast, but by a born writer—a man whose whole being was fixed and concentrated in an astonishing command of words. It is in the multitude of his words that the fertility of Rabelais' spirit most obviously shows itself. His book is an orgy of words; they pour out helter-skelter, wildly, into swirling sentences and huge catalogues that, in serried columns, overflow the page. Not quite wildly, though; for, amid all the rush and bluster, there is a powerful underlying art. The rhythms of this extraordinary prose are long and complex, but they exist; and they are controlled with the absolute skill of a master.

The purpose of Rabelais' book cannot be summed up in a sentence. It may be described as the presentment of a point of view: but *what* point of view? There lies the crux of the question, and numberless critics have wrangled over the solution of it. The truth is, that the only complete description of the point of view is to be found—in the book itself; it is too wide and variegated for any other habitation. Yet, if it would be vain to attempt an accurate and exhaustive account of Rabelais' philosophy, the main outlines of that philosophy are nevertheless visible enough. Alike in the giant-hero, Pantagruel, in his father, Gargantua, and in his follower and boon-companion, Panurge, one can discern the spirit of the Renaissance—expansive, humorous, powerful, and, above all else, alive. Rabelais' book is the incarnation of the great reaction of his epoch against the superstitious gloom and the narrow asceticism of the Middle Ages. He proclaims, in his rich re-echoing voice, a new conception of the world; he denies that it is the vale of sorrows envisioned by the teachers of the past; he declares that it is abounding in glorious energy, abounding in splendid hope, and, by its very nature, good. With a generous hatred of stupidity, he flies full tilt at the pedantic education of the monasteries, and asserts the highest ideals of science and humanity. With an equal loathing of asceticism, he satirizes the monks themselves, and sketches out, in his description of the Abbey of Theleme, a glowing vision of the Utopian convent. His thought was bold; but he lived in a time when the mildest speculation was fraught with danger; and he says what he has to say in the shifting and ambiguous forms of jest and allegory. Yet it was by no means simply for the sake of concealment that he made his work into the singular mixture that it is, of rambling narrative, disconnected incident, capricious disquisition, and coarse humour. That, no doubt, was the very manner in which his mind worked; and the essential element of his spirit resides precisely in this haphazard and various looseness. His exceeding coarseness is itself an expression of one of the most fundamental qualities of his mind—its jovial acceptance of the physical facts of life. Another side of the same characteristic appears in his glorification of eating and drinking: such things were part of the natural constitution of man, therefore let man enjoy them to the full. Who knows? Perhaps the Riddle of the Universe would be solved by the oracle of *la dive Bouteille*.

Rabelais' book is a history of giants, and it is itself gigantic; it is as broad as Gargantua himself. It seems to belong to the morning of the world—a time of mirth, and a time of expectation; when the earth was teeming with a miraculous richness, and the gods walked among men.

In the Essays of MONTAIGNE, written about a generation later, the spirit of the Renaissance, which had filled the pages of Rabelais with such a superabundant energy, appears in a quieter and more cultivated form. The first fine rapture was over; and the impulsive ardours of creative thought were replaced by the calm serenity of criticism and reflection. Montaigne has none of the coarseness, none of the rollicking fun, none of the exuberant optimism, of Rabelais; he is a refined gentleman, who wishes to charm rather than to electrify, who writes in the quiet, easy tone of familiar conversation, who smiles, who broods, and who doubts. The form of the detached essay, which he was the first to use, precisely suited his habit of thought. In that loose shape—admitting of the most indefinite structure, and of any variety of length, from three pages to three hundred—he could say all that he wished to say, in his own desultory, inconsecutive, and unelaborate manner. His book flows on like a prattling brook, winding through pleasant meadows. Everywhere the fruits of wide reading are manifest, and numberless Latin quotations strew his pages. He touches on every side of life—from the slightest and most superficial topics of literature or manners to the profoundest questions that beset humanity; and always with the same tact and happiness, the same wealth of learned illustration, the same engaging grace.

The Essays are concerned fundamentally with two subjects only. First, they illustrate in every variety of way Montaigne's general philosophy of life. That philosophy was an absolutely sceptical one. Amid the mass of conflicting opinions, amid the furious oppositions of creeds, amid the flat contradictions of loudly-asseverated dogmas, Montaigne held a middle course of calm neutrality. *Que Sçais-je?* was his constant motto; and his Essays are a collection of numberless variations on this one dominating theme. The *Apologie de Raimond Sebond*, the largest and the most elaborate of them, contains an immense and searching review of the errors, the incoherences, and the ignorance of humanity, from which Montaigne draws his inevitable conclusion of universal doubt. Whatever the purely philosophical value of this doctrine may be, its importance as an influence in practical life was very great. If no opinion had any certainty whatever, then it followed that persecution for the sake of opinion was simply a wicked folly. Montaigne thus stands out as one of the earliest of the opponents of fanaticism and the apostles of toleration in the history of European thought.

The other subject treated of in the Essays, with an equal persistence and an equal wealth of illustration, is Montaigne himself. The least reticent of writers, he furnishes his readers with every conceivable piece of information concerning his history, his character, his appearance, his health, his habits and his tastes. Here lies the peculiar charm of his book—the endless garrulity of its confidences, which, with their combined humour, suavity, and irresponsibility, bring one right into the intimate presence of a fascinating man.

For this reason, doubtless, no writer has ever been so gushed over as Montaigne; and no writer, we may be sure, would be so horrified as he at such a treatment. Indeed, the adulation of his worshippers has perhaps somewhat obscured the real position that he fills in literature. It is impossible to deny that, both as a writer and as a thinker, he has faults—and grave ones. His style, with all its delightful abundance, its inimitable ease, and its pleasant flavour of antiquity, yet lacks form; he did not possess the supreme mastery of language which alone can lead to the creation of great works of literary art. His scepticism is not important as a contribution to philosophical thought, for his mind was devoid both of the method and of the force necessary for the pursuit and discovery of really significant intellectual truths. To claim for him such titles of distinction is to overshoot the mark, and to distract attention from his true eminence. Montaigne was neither a great artist nor a great philosopher; he was not *great* at all. He was a charming, admirable human being, with the most engaging gift for conversing endlessly and confidentially through the medium of the printed page ever possessed by any man before or after him. Even in his self-revelations he is not profound. How superficial, how insignificant his rambling ingenuous outspokenness appears beside the tremendous introspections of Rousseau! He was probably a better man than Rousseau; he was certainly a more delightful one; but he was far less interesting. It was in the gentle, personal, everyday things of life that his nature triumphed. Here and there in his Essays, this simple goodness wells up clear and pure; and in the wonderful pages on Friendship, one sees, in all its charm and all its sweetness, that beautiful humanity which is the inward essence of Montaigne.

III

THE AGE OF TRANSITION

In the seventy years that elapsed between the death of Montaigne (1592) and the accession to power of Louis XIV the tendencies in French literature were fluctuating and uncertain. It was a period of change, of hesitation, of retrogression even; and yet, below these doubtful, conflicting movements, a great new development was germinating, slowly, surely, and almost unobserved. From one point of view, indeed, this age may be considered the most important in the whole history of the literature, since it prepared the way for the most splendid and characteristic efflorescence in prose and poetry that France has ever known; without it, there would have been no *Grand Siècle*. In fact, it was during this age that the conception was gradually evolved which determined the lines upon which all French literature in the future was to advance. It can hardly be doubted that if the fertile and varied Renaissance movement, which had given birth to the *Pléiade*, to Rabelais, and to Montaigne, had continued to progress unbroken and unchecked, the future literature of France would have closely resembled the contemporary literatures of Spain and England—that it would have continued to be characterized by the experimental boldness and the loose exuberance of the masters of the sixteenth century. But in France the movement *was* checked: and the result was a body of literature, not only of the highest value, but also of a unique significance in European letters.

The break in the Renaissance movement was largely the result of political causes. The stability and peace which seemed to be so firmly established by the brilliant monarchy of Francis I vanished with the terrible outbreak of the Wars of Religion. For about sixty years, with a few intermissions, the nation was a prey to the horrors of civil strife. And when at last order was restored under the powerful rule of Cardinal Richelieu, and the art of writing began to be once more assiduously practised, the fresh rich glory of the Renaissance spirit had irrevocably passed away. Already, early in the seventeenth century, the poetry of MALHERBE had given expression to new theories and new ideals. A man of powerful though narrow intelligence, a passionate theorist, and an ardent specialist in grammar and the use of words, Malherbe reacted violently both against the misplaced and artificial erudition of the *Pléiade* and their unforced outbursts of lyric song. His object was to purify the French tongue; to make it—even at the cost of diminishing its flavour and narrowing its range—strong, supple, accurate and correct; to create a language which, though it might be incapable of expressing the fervours of personal passion or the airy fancies of dreamers, would be a perfect instrument for the enunciation of noble truths and fine imaginations, in forms at once simple, splendid and sincere. Malherbe's importance lies rather in his influence than in his actual work. Some of his Odes—among which his great address to Louis XIII on the rebellion of La Rochelle deserves the highest place—are admirable examples of a restrained, measured and weighty rhetoric, moving to the music not of individual emotion, but of a generalized feeling for the beauty and grandeur of high thoughts. He was essentially an oratorical poet; but unfortunately the only forms of verse ready to his hand were lyrical forms; so that his genius never found a full scope for its powers. Thus his precept outweighs his example. His poetical theories found their full justification only in the work of his greater and more fortunate successors; and the masters of the age of Louis XIV looked back to Malherbe as the intellectual father of their race.

Malherbe's immediate influence, however, was very limited. Upon the generation of writers that followed him, his doctrines of sobriety and simplicity made no impression whatever. Their tastes lay in an entirely different direction. For now, in the second quarter of the seventeenth century, there set in, with an extreme and sudden violence, a fashion for every kind of literary contortion, affectation and trick. The value of a poet was measured by his capacity for turning a somersault in verse—for constructing ingenious word-puzzles with which to express exaggerated sentiments; and no prose-writer was worth looking at who could not drag a complicated, ramifying simile through half a dozen pages at least. These artificialities lacked the saving grace of those of the Renaissance writers—their abounding vigour and their inventive skill. They were cold-blooded artificialities, evolved elaborately, simply for their own sake. The new school, with its twisted conceits and its super-subtle elegances, came to be known as the 'Precious' school, and it is under that name that the satire of subsequent writers has handed it down to the laughter of after-generations. Yet a perspicacious eye might have seen even in these absurd and tasteless productions the signs of a progressive movement—the possibility, at least, of a true advance. For the contortions of the 'Precious' writers were less the result of their inability to write well than of their desperate efforts to do so. They were trying, as hard as they could, to wriggle themselves into a beautiful pose; and, naturally enough, they were unsuccessful. They were, in short, too self-conscious; but it was in this very self-consciousness that the real hope for the future lay. The teaching of Malherbe, if it did not influence the actual form of their work, at least impelled them towards a deliberate effort to produce *some* form, and to be content no longer with the vague and the haphazard. In two directions particularly this new self-consciousness showed itself. It showed itself in the formation of literary *salons*—of which the chief was the famous blue drawing-room of the Hôtel de Rambouillet—where every conceivable question of taste and art, grammar and vocabulary, was discussed with passionate intensity; and it showed itself even more strongly in the establishment, under the influence of Richelieu, of an official body of literary experts—the French Academy.

How far the existence of the Academy has influenced French literature, either for good or for evil, is an extremely dubious question. It was formed for the purpose of giving fixity and correctness to the language, of preserving a high standard of literary taste, and of creating an authoritative centre from which the ablest men of letters of the day should radiate their influence over the country. To a great extent these ends have been attained; but they have been accompanied by corresponding drawbacks. Such an institution must necessarily be a conservative one; and it is possible that the value of the Academy as a centre of purity and taste has been at least balanced by the extreme reluctance which it has always shown to countenance any of those forms of audacity and change without which no literature can be saved from petrifaction. All through its history the Academy has been timid and out of date. The result has been that some of the very greatest of French writers—including Molière, Diderot, and Flaubert—have remained outside it; while all the most fruitful developments in French literary theory have come about only after a bitter and desperate resistance on its part. On the whole, perhaps the most important function performed by the Academy has been a more indirect one. The mere existence of a body of writers officially recognized by the authorities of the State has undoubtedly given a peculiar prestige to the profession of letters in France. It has emphasized that tendency to take the art of writing seriously—to regard it as a fit object for the most conscientious craftsmanship and deliberate care—which is so characteristic of French writers. The amateur is very rare in French literature—as rare as he is common in our own. How many of the greatest English writers have denied that they were men of letters!—Scott, Byron, Gray, Sir Thomas Browne, perhaps even Shakespeare himself. When Congreve begged Voltaire not to talk of literature, but to regard him merely as an English gentleman, the French writer, who, in all his multifarious activities, never forgot for a moment that he was first and foremost a follower of the profession of letters, was overcome with astonishment and disgust. The difference is typical of the attitude of the two nations towards literature: the English, throwing off their glorious masterpieces by the way, as if they were trifles; and the French bending all the resources of a trained and patient energy to the construction and the perfection of marvellous works of art.

Whatever view we may take of the ultimate influence of the French Academy, there can be no doubt at all that one of its first actions was singularly inauspicious. Under the guidance of Cardinal Richelieu it delivered a futile attack upon the one writer who stood out head and shoulders above his contemporaries, and whose works bore all the marks of unmistakable genius—the great CORNEILLE. With the production, in 1636, of Corneille's tragedy, *Le Cid*, modern French drama came into existence. Previous to that date, two main movements are discernible in French dramatic art—one carrying on the medieval traditions of the mystery-and miracle-play, and culminating, early in the seventeenth century, with the rough, vigorous and popular drama of Hardy; and the other, originating with the writers of the Renaissance, and leading to the production of a number of learned and literary plays, composed in strict imitation of the tragedies of Seneca,—plays of which the typical representative is the *Cléopâtre* of Jodelle. Corneille's achievement was based upon a combination of what was best in these two movements. The work of Jodelle, written with a genuinely artistic intention, was nevertheless a dead thing on the stage; while Hardy's melodramas, bursting as they were with vitality, were too barbaric to rank as serious works of art. Corneille combined art with vitality, and for the first time produced a play which was at once a splended piece of literature and an immense popular success. Henceforward it was certain that French drama would develop along the path which had been opened out for it so triumphantly by the *Cid*. But what was that path?

Nothing shows more strikingly the strength of the literary opinion of that age than the fact that it was able to impose itself even upon the mighty and towering spirit of Corneille. By nature, there can be little doubt that Corneille was a romantic. His fiery energy, his swelling rhetoric, his love of the extraordinary and the sublime, bring him into closer kinship with Marlowe than with any other writer of his own nation until the time of Victor Hugo. But Corneille could not do what Marlowe did. He could not infuse into the free form of popular drama the passion and splendour of his own genius, and thus create a type of tragedy that was at once exuberant and beautiful. And he could not do this because the literary theories of the whole of the cultivated society of France would have been opposed to him, because he himself was so impregnated with those very theories that he failed to realize where the true bent of his genius lay. Thus it was that the type of drama which he impressed upon French literature was not the romantic type of the English Elizabethans, but the classical type of Senecan tragedy which Jodelle had imitated, and which was alone tolerable to the French critics of the seventeenth century. Instead of making the vital drama of Hardy artistic, he made the literary drama of Jodelle alive. Probably it was fortunate that he did so; for he thus led the way straight to the most characteristic product of the French genius—the tragedy of Racine. With Racine, the classical type of drama, which so ill befitted the romantic spirit of Corneille, found its perfect exponent; and it will be well therefore to postpone a more detailed examination of the nature of that type until we come to consider Racine himself, the value of whose work is inextricably interwoven with its form. The dominating qualities of Corneille may be more easily appreciated.

He was above all things a rhetorician; he was an instinctive master of those qualities in words which go to produce effects of passionate vehemence, vigorous precision, and culminating force. His great *tirades* carry forward the reader, or the listener (for indeed the verse of Corneille loses half its value when it is unheard), on a full-flowing tide of language where the waves of the verse, following one another in a swift succession of ever-rising power, crash down at last with a roar. It is a strange kind of poetry: not that of imaginative vision, of plastic beauty, of subtle feeling; but that of intellectual excitement and spiritual strength. It is the poetry of Malherbe multiplied a thousandfold in vigour and in genius, and expressed in the form most appropriate to it—the dramatic Alexandrine verse. The stuff out of which it is woven, made up, not of the images of sense, but of the processes of thought, is, in fact, simply argument. One can understand how verse created from such material might be vigorous and impressive; it is difficult to imagine how it could also be passionate—until one has read Corneille. Then one realizes afresh the compelling power of genius. His tragic personages, standing forth without mystery, without 'atmosphere', without local colour, but simply in the clear white light of reason, rivet our attention, and seem at last to seize upon our very souls. Their sentences, balanced, weighty and voluble, reveal the terrors of destiny, the furies of love, the exasperations of pride, with an intensity of intellectual precision that burns and blazes. The deeper these strange beings sink into their anguish, the more remorseless their arguments become. They prove their horror in dreadful syllogisms; every inference plunges them farther into the abyss; and their intelligence flames upward to its highest point, when they are finally engulfed.

Such is the singular passion that fills Corneille's tragedies. The creatures that give utterance to it are hardly human beings: they are embodiments of will, force, intellect and pride. The situations in which they are placed are calculated to expose these qualities to the utmost; and all Corneille's masterpieces are concerned with the same subject—the combat between indomitable egoism and the forces of Fate. It is in the meeting of these 'fell incensed opposites' that the tragedy consists. In *Le Cid*, Chimene's passion for Rodrigue struggles in a death-grapple with the destiny that makes Rodrigue the slayer of her father. In *Polyeucte* it is the same passion struggling with the dictates of religion. In *Les Horaces*, patriotism, family love and personal passion are all pitted against Fate. In *Cinna*, the conflict passes within the mind of Auguste, between the promptings of a noble magnanimity and the desire for revenge. In all these plays the central characters display a superhuman courage and constancy and self-control. They are ideal figures, speaking with a force and an elevation unknown in actual experience; they never blench, they never waver, but move adamantine to their doom. They are for ever asserting the strength of their own individuality.

> *Je suis maître de moi comme de l'univers,*
> *Je le suis, je veux l'être,*

declares Auguste; and Médée, at the climax of her misfortunes, uses the same language—

'Dans un si grand revers que vous reste-t-il?'—'Moi!
Moi, dis-je, et c'est assez!'

The word 'moi' dominates these tragedies; and their heroes, bursting with this extraordinary egoism, assume even more towering proportions in their self-abnegation than in their pride. Then the thrilling clarion-notes of their defiances give way to the deep grand music of stern sublimity and stoic resignation. The gigantic spirit recoils upon itself, crushes itself, and reaches its last triumph.

Drama of this kind must, it is clear, lack many of the qualities which are usually associated with the dramatic art; there is no room in it for variety of character-drawing, for delicacy of feeling, or for the realistic presentation of the experiences of life. Corneille hardly attempted to produce such effects as these; and during his early years his great gifts of passion and rhetoric easily made up for the deficiency. As he grew older, however, his inspiration weakened; his command of his material left him; and he was no longer able to fill the figures of his creation with the old intellectual sublimity. His heroes and his heroines became mere mouthing puppets, pouring out an endless stream of elaborate, high-flown sentiments, wrapped up in a complicated jargon of argumentative verse. His later plays are miserable failures. Not only do they illustrate the inherent weaknesses of Corneille's dramatic method, but they are also full of the characteristic bad taste and affectations of the age. The vital spirit once withdrawn, out sprang the noisome creatures from their lurking-places to feast upon the corpse.

Nevertheless, with all his faults, Corneille dominated French literature for twenty years. His genius, transcendent, unfortunate, noble in endeavour, unequal in accomplishment, typifies the ambiguous movement of the time. For still the flood of 'Precious' literature poured from the press—dull, contorted epics, and stilted epigrams on my lady's eyebrow, and learned dissertations decked out in sparkling tinsel, and infinitely long romances, full of alembicated loves. Then suddenly one day a small pamphlet in the form of a letter appeared on the bookstalls of Paris; and with its appearance the long reign of confused ideals and misguided efforts came to an end for ever. The pamphlet was the first of Pascal's *Lettres Provinciales*—the work which ushered into being the great classical age—the *Grand Siècle* of Louis XIV.

In the *Lettres Provinciales* PASCAL created French prose—the French prose that we know to-day, the French prose which ranks by virtue of its vigour, elegance and precision as a unique thing in the literature of the world. Earlier prose-writers—Joinville, Froissart, Rabelais, Montaigne—had been in turns charming, or picturesque, or delicate, or overflowing with vitality; but none had struck upon the really characteristically French note. They lacked form, and those fine qualities of strength and clarity which form alone can give. Their sentences were indeterminate—long, complex, drifting, and connected together by conjunctions into a loose aggregate. The 'Precious' writers had dimly realized the importance of form, but they had not realized at all the importance of simplicity. This was Pascal's great discovery. His sentences are clear, straightforward, and distinct; and they are bound together into a succession of definitely articulated paragraphs, which are constructed, not on the system of mere haphazard aggregation, but according to the logical development of the thought. Thus Pascal's prose, like the verse of Malherbe and Corneille, is based upon reason; it is primarily intellectual. But, with Pascal, the intellect expresses itself even more exactly. The last vestiges of medieval ambiguities have been discarded; the style is perfectly modern. So wonderfully did Pascal master the resources of the great instrument which he had forged, that it is true to say that no reader who wishes to realize once for all the great qualities of French prose could do better than turn straight to the *Lettres Provinciales*. Here he will find the lightness and the strength, the exquisite polish and the delicious wit, the lambent irony and the ordered movement, which no other language spoken by man has ever quite been able to produce. The *Lettres* are a work of controversy; their actual subject-matter—the ethical system of the Jesuits of the time—is remote from modern interests; yet such is the brilliance of Pascal's art that every page of them is fascinating to-day. The vivacity of the opening letters is astonishing; the tone is the gay, easy tone of a man of the world; the attack is delivered in a rushing onslaught of raillery. Gradually, as the book proceeds, there are signs of a growing seriousness; we have a sense of graver issues, and round the small question of the Jesuits' morality we discern ranged all the vast forces of good and evil. At last the veil of wit and laughter is entirely removed, and Pascal bursts forth into the full fury of invective. The vials of wrath are opened; a terrific denunciation rolls out in a thundering cataract; and at the close of the book there is hardly a note in the whole gamut of language, from the airiest badinage to the darkest objurgation, which has not been touched.

In sheer genius Pascal ranks among the very greatest writers who have lived upon this earth. And his genius was not simply artistic; it displayed itself no less in his character and in the quality of his thought. These are the sides of him which are revealed with extraordinary splendour in his *Pensées*—a collection of notes intended to form the basis for an elaborate treatise in defence of Christianity which Pascal did not live to complete. The style of many of these passages surpasses in brilliance and force even that of the *Lettres Provinciales*. In addition, one hears the intimate voice of Pascal, speaking upon the profoundest problems of existence—the most momentous topics which can agitate the minds of men. Two great themes compose his argument: the miserable insignificance of all that is human—human reason, human knowledge, human ambition; and the transcendent glory of God. Never was the wretchedness of mankind painted with a more passionate power. The whole infinitude of the physical universe is invoked in his sweeping sentences to crush the presumption of man. Man's intellectual greatness itself he seizes upon to point the moral of an innate contradiction, an essential imbecility. 'Quelle chimère,' he exclaims, 'est-ce donc que l'homme! quelle nouveauté, quel monstre, quel chaos, quel sujet de contradiction, quel prodige! Juge de toutes choses, imbécile ver de terre, dépositaire du vrai, cloaque d'incertitude et d'erreur, gloire et rebut de l'univers!' In words of imperishable intensity, he dwells upon the omnipotence of Death: 'Nous sommes plaisants de nous reposer dans la société de nos semblables. Misérables comme nous, impuissants comme nous, ils ne nous aideront pas; on mourra seul.' Or he summons up in one ghastly sentence the vision of the inevitable end: 'Le dernier acte est sanglant, quelque belle que soit la comédie en tout le reste. On jette enfin de la terre sur la tête, et en voilà pour jamais.' And so follows the conclusion of the whole: 'Connaissez donc, superbe, quel paradoxe vous êtes à vous-même. Humiliez-vous, raison impuissante; taisez-vous, nature imbécile. . . et entendez de votre maître votre condition véritable que vous ignorez. Écoutez Dieu.'

Modern as the style of Pascal's writing is, his thought is deeply impregnated with the spirit of the Middle Ages. He belonged, almost equally, to the future and to the past. He was a distinguished man of science, a brilliant mathematician; yet he shrank from a consideration of the theory of Copernicus: it was more important, he declared, to think of the immortal soul. In the last years of his short life he sank into a torpor of superstition—ascetic, self-mortified, and rapt in a strange exaltation, like a medieval monk. Thus there is a tragic antithesis in his character—an unresolved discord which shows itself again and again in his *Pensées*. 'Condition de l'homme,' he notes, 'inconstance, ennui, inquiétude.' It is the description of his own state. A profound inquietude did indeed devour him. He turned desperately from the pride of his intellect to the consolations of his religion. But even there—? Beneath him, as he sat or as he walked, a great gulf seemed to open darkly, into an impenetrable abyss. He looked upward into heaven, and the familiar horror faced him still: 'Le silence éternel de ces espaces infinis m'effraie!'

IV

The Age of Louis XIV

When Louis XIV assumed the reins of government France suddenly and wonderfully came to her maturity; it was as if the whole nation had burst into splendid flower. In every branch of human activity—in war, in administration, in social life, in art, and in literature—the same energy was apparent, the same glorious success. At a bound France won the headship of Europe; and when at last, defeated in arms and politically shattered, she was forced to relinquish her dreams of worldly power, her pre-eminence in the arts of peace remained unshaken. For more than a century she continued, through her literature and her manners, to dominate the civilized world.

At no other time have the conditions of society exercised a more profound influence upon the works of great writers. Though, with the ascendancy of Louis, the political power of the nobles finally came to an end, France remained, in the whole complexion of her social life, completely aristocratic. Louis, with deliberate policy, emphasized the existing rigidity of class-distinctions by centralizing society round his splendid palace of Versailles. Versailles is the *clou* to the age of Louis XIV. The huge, almost infinite building, so stately and so glorious, with its vast elaborate gardens, its great trees transported from distant forests, its amazing waterworks constructed in an arid soil at the cost of millions, its lesser satellite parks and palaces, its palpitating crowds of sumptuous courtiers, the whole accumulated mass of piled-up treasure and magnificence and power—this was something far more significant than the mere country residence of royalty; it was the summary, the crown, and the visible expression of the ideals of a great age. And what were these ideals? The fact that the conception of society which made Versailles possible was narrow and unjust must not blind us to the real nobility and the real glory which it brought into being. It is true that behind and beyond the radiance of Louis and his courtiers lay the dark abyss of an impoverished France, a ruined peasantry, a whole system of intolerance, and privilege, and maladministration; yet it is none the less true that the radiance was a genuine radiance—no false and feeble glitter, but the warm, brilliant, intense illumination thrown out by the glow of a nation's life. That life, with all it meant to those who lived it, has long since vanished from the earth—preserved to us now only in the pages of its poets, or strangely shadowed forth to the traveller in the illimitable desolation of Versailles. That it has gone so utterly is no doubt, on the whole, a cause for rejoicing; but, as we look back upon it, we may still feel something of the old enchantment, and feel it, perhaps, the more keenly for its strangeness—its dissimilarity to the experiences of our own days. We shall catch glimpses of a world of pomp and brilliance, of ceremony and decoration, a small, vital passionate world which has clothed itself in ordered beauty, learnt a fine way of easy, splendid living, and come under the spell of a devotion to what is, to us, no more than the gorgeous phantom of high imaginations—the divinity of a king. When the morning sun was up and the horn was sounding down the long avenues, who would not wish, if only in fancy, to join the glittering cavalcade where the young Louis led the hunt in the days of his opening glory? Later, we might linger on the endless terrace, to watch the great monarch, with his red heels and his golden snuff-box and his towering periwig, come out among his courtiers, or in some elaborate grotto applaud a ballet by Molière. When night fell there would be dancing and music in the gallery blazing with a thousand looking-glasses, or masquerades and feasting in the gardens, with the torches throwing strange shadows among the trees trimmed into artificial figures, and gay lords and proud ladies conversing together under the stars.

Such were the surroundings among which the classical literature of France came into existence, and by which it was profoundly influenced in a multitude of ways. This literature was, in its form and its essence, aristocratic literature, though its writers were, almost without exception, middle-class men brought into prominence by the royal favour. The great dramatists and poets and prose-writers of the epoch were in the position of artists working by special permission for the benefit and pleasure of a select public to which they themselves had no claim to belong. They were *in* the world of high birth and splendid manners, but they were not of it; and thus it happened that their creations, while reflecting what was finest in the social ideals of the time, escaped the worst faults of the literary productions of persons of rank—superficiality and amateurishness. The literature of that age was, in fact, remarkable to an extraordinary degree for precisely contrary qualities—for the solidity of its psychological foundations and for the supreme excellence of its craftsmanship. It was the work of profound and subtle artists writing for a small, leisured, distinguished, and critical audience, while retaining the larger outlook and sense of proportion which had come to them from their own experience of life.

The fact, too, that this aristocratic audience was no longer concerned with the activities of political power, exercised a further influence upon the writers of the age. The old interests of aristocracy—the romance of action, the exalted passions of chivalry and war—faded into the background, and their place was taken by the refined and intimate pursuits of peace and civilization. The exquisite letters of Madame de Sévigné show us society assuming its modern complexion, women becoming the arbiters of taste and fashion, and drawing-rooms the centre of life. These tendencies were reflected in literature; and Corneille's tragedies of power were replaced by Racine's tragedies of the heart. Nor was it only in the broad outlines that the change was manifest; the whole temper of life, in all its details, took on the suave, decorous, dignified tone of good breeding, and it was impossible that men of letters should escape the infection. Their works became remarkable for clarity and elegance, for a graceful simplicity, an easy strength; they were cast in the fine mould of perfect manners—majestic without pretension, expressive without emphasis, simple without carelessness, and subtle without affectation. These are the dominating qualities in the style of that great body of literature, which has rightly come to be distinguished as the *Classical* literature of France.

Yet there was a reverse to the medal; for such qualities necessarily involved defects, which, hardly perceptible and of small importance in the work of the early masters of the Classical school, became more prominent in the hands of lesser men, and eventually brought the whole tradition into disrepute. It was inevitable that there should be a certain narrowness in a literature which was in its very essence deliberate, refined, and select; omission is the beginning of all art; and the great French classicists, more supremely artistic, perhaps, than any other body of writers in the history of the world, practised with unsparing devotion the virtue of leaving out. The beauties of clarity, simplicity, and ease were what they aimed at; and to attain them involved the abandonment of other beauties which, however attractive, were incompatible with those. Vague suggestion, complexity of thought, strangeness of imagination—to us the familiar ornaments of poetry—were qualities eschewed by the masters of the age of Louis XIV. They were willing to forgo comprehensiveness and elaboration, they were ready to forswear the great effects of curiosity and mystery; for the pursuit of these led away from the high path of their chosen endeavour—the creation, within the limits they had marked out, of works of flawless art. The fact that they succeeded so well is precisely one of the reasons why it is difficult for the modern reader—and for the Anglo-Saxon one especially, with his different æsthetic traditions—to appreciate their work to the full. To us, with our broader outlook, our more complicated interests, our more elusive moods, their small bright world is apt to seem uninteresting and out of date, unless we spend some patient sympathy in the discovery of the real charm and the real beauty that it contains. Nor is this our only difficulty: the classical tradition, like all traditions, became degenerate; its virtues hardened into mannerisms, its weaknesses expanded into dogmas; and it is sometimes hard for us to discriminate between the artist who has mastered the convention in which he works, and the artisan who is the slave of it. The convention itself, if it is unfamiliar to us, is what fills our attention, so that we forget to look for the moving spirit behind. And indeed, in the work of the later classicists, there was too often no spirit to look for. The husk alone remained—a finicky pretentious framework, fluttering with the faded rags of ideals long outworn. Every great tradition has its own way of dying; and the classical tradition died of timidity. It grew afraid of the flesh and blood of life; it was too polite to face realities, too elevated to tread the common ground of fact and detail; it would touch nothing but generalities, for they alone are safe, harmless, and respectable; and, if they are also empty, how can that he helped? Starving, it shrank into itself, muttering old incantations; and it continued to mutter them, automatically, some time after it had expired.

But, in the heyday of the age of Louis XIV, literature showed no signs of such a malady—though no doubt it contained the latent germs of the disease; on the contrary, the masterpieces of that epoch are charged to the full with vitality and force. We may describe them, in one word, as worldly—worldly in the broadest and the highest acceptation of the term. They represent, in its perfect expression, the spirit of this world—its greatness, its splendour, its intensity, the human drama that animates it, the ordered beauty towards which it tends. For that was an age in which the world, in all the plenitude of its brilliance, had come into its own, when the sombre spirituality of the Middle Ages had been at last forgotten, when the literatures of Greece and Rome had delivered their benignant message, when civilization could enjoy for a space its new maturity, before a larger vision had brought questionings, and an inward vision aspirations unknown before. The literature of those days was founded upon a general acceptance—acceptance both in the sphere of politics and of philosophy. It took for granted a fixed and autocratic society; it silently assumed the orthodox teaching of the Roman Catholic Church. Thus, compared with the literature of the eighteenth century, it was unspeculative; compared with that of the Middle Ages, unspiritual. It was devoid of that perception of the marvellous and awful significance of Natural phenomena which dominates the literature of the Romantic Revival. Fate, Eternity, Nature, the destiny of Man, 'the prophetic soul of the wide world dreaming on things to come'— such mysteries it almost absolutely ignored. Even Death seemed to lie a little beyond its vision. What a difference, in this respect, between the literature of Louis XIV and the literature of Elizabeth! The latter is obsessed by the smell of mortality; its imagination, penetrating to the depths and the heights, shows us mankind adrift amid eternities, and the whole universe the doubtful shadow of a dream. In the former, these magnificent obscurities find no place: they have been shut out, as it were, like a night of storm and darkness on the other side of the window. The night is there, no doubt; but it is outside, invisible and neglected, while within, the candles are lighted, the company is gathered together, and all is warmth and brilliance. To eyes which have grown accustomed to the elemental conflicts without, the room may seem at first confined, artificial, and insignificant. But let us wait a little! Gradually we shall come to feel the charm of the well-ordered chamber, to appreciate the beauty of the decorations, the distinction and the penetration of the talk. And, if we persevere, that is not all we shall discover. We shall find, in that small society, something more than ease and good breeding and refinement; we shall find the play of passion and the subtle manifestation of the soul; we shall realize that the shutting out of terrors and of mysteries has brought at least the gain of concentration, so that we may discern unhindered the movements of the mind of man—of man, not rapt aloft in the vast ardours of speculation, nor involved in the solitary introspection of his own breast; but of man, civilized, actual, among his fellows, in the bright light of the world.

Yet, if it is true that a refined and splendid worldliness was the dominant characteristic of the literature of the age, it is no less true that here and there, in its greatest writers, a contrary tendency—faint but unmistakable—may be perceived. The tone occasionally changes; below the polished surface a disquietude becomes discernible; a momentary obscure exception to the general easy-flowing rule. The supreme artists of the epoch seem to have been able not only to give expression to the moving forces of their time, but to react against them. They were rebels as well as conquerors, and this fact lends an extraordinary interest to their work. Like some subtle unexpected spice in a masterly confection, a strange, profound, unworldly melancholy just permeates their most brilliant writings, and gives the last fine taste.

Before considering these supreme artists more particularly, it will be well to notice briefly the work of one who can lay no claim to such a title, but who deserves attention as the spokesman of the literary ideals of his age. BOILEAU, once the undisputed arbiter of taste throughout Europe, is now hardly remembered save as the high-priest of an effete tradition and as the author of some brilliant lines which have passed as proverbs into the French language. He was a man of vivid intelligence—courageous, independent, passionately devoted to literature, and a highly skilled worker in the difficult art of writing verse. But he lacked the force and the finesse of poetic genius; and it is not as a poet that he is interesting: it is as a critic. When the lines upon which French literature was to develop were still uncertain, when the Classical school was in its infancy, and its great leaders—Molière, Racine, La Fontaine—were still disputing their right to pre-eminence among a host of inferior and now forgotten writers whose works were carrying on the weak and tasteless traditions of the former age—it was at this moment that Boileau brought to the aid of the new movement the whole force of his admirable clear-sightedness, his dauntless pertinacity, and his caustic, unforgettable wit. No doubt, without him, the Classical school would have triumphed—ultimately, like all good things—but it would be hard to exaggerate the service which was rendered it by Boileau. During many years, in a long series of satires and epistles, in the *Art Poétique* and in various prose works, he impressed upon the reading public the worthlessness of the old artificial school of preciosity and affectation, and the high value of the achievements of his great contemporaries. He did more: he not only attacked and eulogized the works of individuals, he formulated general principles and gave pointed and repeated expression to the ideals of the new school. Thus, through him, classicism gained self-consciousness; it became possessed of a definite doctrine; and a group of writers was formed, united together by common aims, and destined to exercise an immense influence upon the development not only of French, but of European literature. For these reasons—for his almost unerring prescience in the discernment of contemporary merit and for his triumphant consolidation of the classical tradition—Boileau must be reckoned as the earliest of that illustrious company of great critics which is one of the peculiar glories of French letters. The bulk of his writing will probably never again be read by any save the curious explorer; but the spirit of his work lies happily condensed in one short epistle—*À son Esprit*—where his good sense, his wit, his lucid vigour and his essential humanity find their consummate expression; it is a spirit which still animates the literature of France.

His teaching, however, so valuable in its own day, is not important as a contribution towards a general theory of æsthetics. Boileau attempted to lay down the principles universally binding upon writers of poetry; but he had not the equipment necessary for such a task. His knowledge was limited, his sympathies were narrow, and his intellectual powers lacked profundity. The result was that he committed the common fault of writers immersed in the business of contemporary controversy—he erected the precepts, which he saw to be salutary so far as his own generation was concerned, to the dignity of universal rules. His message, in reality, was for the France of Louis XIV; he enunciated it as if it was the one guide to literary salvation for all ages and in all circumstances; and it so happened that for about a century it was accepted at his own valuation by the majority of civilized mankind. Boileau detested—and rightly detested—the extravagant affectations of the *précieux* school, the feeble pomposities of Chapelain, the contorted, inflated, logic-chopping heroes of Corneille's later style; and the classical reaction against these errors appeared to him in the guise of a return to the fundamental principles of Nature, Reason, and Truth. In a sense he was right: for it is certain that the works of Molière and Racine were more natural, more reasonable, and more truthful than those of l'Abbé Cotin and Pradon; his mistake lay in his assumption that these qualities were the monopoly of the Classical school. Perceiving the beauty of clarity, order, refinement, and simplicity, he jumped to the conclusion that these were the characteristics of Nature herself, and that without them no beauty could exist. He was wrong. Nature is too large a thing to fit into a system of aesthetics; and beauty is often—perhaps more often than not—complex, obscure, fantastic, and strange. At the bottom of all Boileau's theories lay a hearty love of sound common sense. It was not, as has sometimes been asserted, imagination that he disliked, but singularity. He could write, for instance, an enthusiastic appreciation of the sublime sentence, 'God said, Let there be light, and there was light'; for there imagination is clothed in transparent beauty, and grandeur is achieved by the simplest means. More completely than any of his great contemporaries, Boileau was a representative of middle-class France.

Certainly the most famous, and perhaps the greatest, of the writers for whom Boileau acted as the apologist and the interpreter was Molière. In the literature of France Molière occupies the same kind of position as Cervantes in that of Spain, Dante in that of Italy, and Shakespeare in that of England. His glory is more than national—it is universal. Gathering within the plenitude of his genius the widest and the profoundest characteristics of his race, he has risen above the boundaries of place and language and tradition into a large dominion over the hearts of all mankind. To the world outside France he alone, in undisputed eminence, speaks with the authentic voice of France herself.

That this is so is owing mainly, of course, to the power of his genius; but it is also owing, in some degree, to the particular form which his genius took. Judging by quality alone, it is difficult to say whether his work stands higher or lower in the scale of human achievement than that of Racine—whether the breadth of vision, the diversity, and the humanity of his comedies do or do not counterbalance the poetry, the intensity, and the perfect art of his friend's tragedies; at least it seems certain that the difference between the reputations of the two men with the world in general by no means corresponds with the real difference in their worth. It is by his very perfection, by the very completeness of his triumph, that Racine loses. He is so absolute, so special a product of French genius, that it is well-nigh impossible for any one not born a Frenchman to appreciate him to the full; it is by his incompleteness, and to some extent even by his imperfections, that Molière gains. Of all the great French classics, he is the least classical. His fluid mind overflowed the mould he worked in. His art, sweeping over the whole range of comic emotions, from the wildest buffoonery to the grimmest satire and the subtlest wit, touched life too closely and too often to attain to that flawless beauty to which it seems to aspire. He lacked the precision of form which is the mark of the consummate artist; he was sometimes tentative and ambiguous, often careless; the structure of some of his finest works was perfunctorily thrown together; the envelope of his thought—his language—was by no means faultless, his verse often coming near to prose, and his prose sometimes aping the rhythm of verse. In fact, it is not surprising that to the rigid classicists of the eighteenth century this Colossus had feet of clay. But, after all, even clay has a merit of its own: it is the substance of the common earth. That substance, entering into the composition of Molière, gave him his broad-based solidity, and brought him into kinship with the wide humanity of the world.

It was on this side that his work was profoundly influenced by the circumstances of his life. Molière never knew the leisure, the seclusion, the freedom from external cares, without which it is hardly possible for art to mature to perfection; he passed his existence in the thick of the battle, and he died as he had lived—in the harness of the professional entertainer. His early years were spent amid the rough and sordid surroundings of a travelling provincial company, of which he became the manager and the principal actor, and for which he composed his first plays. He matured late. It was not till he was thirty-seven that he produced *Les Précieuses Ridicules*—his first work of genius; and it was not till three years later that he came into the full possession of his powers with *L'École des Femmes*. All his masterpieces were written in the ten years that followed (1662–73). During that period the patronage of the king gave him an assured position; he became a celebrity at Paris and Versailles; he was a successful man. Yet, even during these years of prosperity, he was far from being free from troubles. He was obliged to struggle incessantly against the intrigues of his enemies, among whom the ecclesiastical authorities were the most ferocious; and even the favour of Louis had its drawbacks, for it involved a constant expenditure of energy upon the frivolous and temporary entertainments of the Court. In addition, he was unhappy in his private life. Unlike Shakespeare, with whom his career offers many analogies, he never lived to reap the quiet benefit of his work, for he died in the midst of it, at the age of fifty-one, after a performance in the title-rôle of his own *Malade Imaginaire*.

What he had achieved was, in the first place, the creation of French Comedy. Before him, there had been boisterous farces, conventional comedies of intrigue borrowed from the Italian, and extravagant pieces of adventure and burlesque cast in the Spanish mould. Molière did for the comic element in French literature what Corneille had done for the tragic: he raised it to the level of serious art. It was he who first completely discovered the æsthetic possibilities that lay in the ordinary life of every day. He was the most unromantic of writers—a realist to the core; and he understood that the true subject of comedy was to be found in the actual facts of human society—in the affectations of fools, the absurdities of cranks, the stupidities of dupes, the audacities of impostors, the humours and the follies of family life. And, like all great originators, his influence has been immense. At one blow, he established Comedy in its true position and laid down the lines on which it was to develop for the next two hundred years. At the present day, all over Europe, the main characteristics of the average play may be traced straight back to their source in the dominating genius of Molière.

If he fell short of the classical ideal in his workmanship, if he exceeded it in the breadth and diversity of his mind, it is still true that the essence of his dramatic method was hardly less classical than that of Racine himself. His subject-matter was rich and various; but his treatment of it was strictly limited by the classical conception of art. He always worked by selection. His incidents are very few, chosen with the utmost care, impressed upon the spectator with astonishing force, and exquisitely arranged to succeed each other at the most effective moment. The choice of the incidents is determined invariably by one consideration—the light which they throw upon the characters; and the characters themselves appear to us from only a very few carefully chosen points of view. The narrowed and selective nature of Molière's treatment of character presents an illuminating contrast when compared with the elaborately detailed method of such a master of the romantic style as Shakespeare. The English dramatist shows his persons to us in the round; innumerable facets flash out quality after quality; the subtlest and most elusive shades of temperament are indicated; until at last the whole being takes shape before us, endowed with what seems to be the very complexity and mystery of life itself. Entirely different is the great Frenchman's way. Instead of expanding, he deliberately narrows his view; he seizes upon two or three salient qualities in a character and then uses all his art to impress them indelibly upon our minds. His Harpagon is a miser, and he is old—and that is all we know about him: how singularly limited a presentment compared with that of Shakespeare's bitter, proud, avaricious, vindictive, sensitive, and almost pathetic Jew! Tartufe, perhaps the greatest of all Molière's characters, presents a less complex figure even than such a slight sketch as Shakespeare's Malvolio. Who would have foreseen Malvolio's exquisitely preposterous address to Jove? In Tartufe there are no such surprises. He displays three qualities, and three only—religious hypocrisy, lasciviousness, and the love of power; and there is not a word that he utters which is not impregnated with one or all of these. Beside the vast elaboration of a Falstaff he seems, at first sight, hardly more solid than some astounding silhouette; yet—such was the power and intensity of Molière's art—the more we look, the more difficult we shall find it to be certain that Tartufe is a less tremendous creation even than Falstaff himself.

For, indeed, it is in his characters that Molière's genius triumphs most. His method is narrow, but it is deep. He rushes to the essentials of a human being—tears out his vitals, as it were—and, with a few repeated master-strokes, transfixes the naked soul. His flashlight never fails: the affected fop, the ignorant doctor, the silly tradesman, the heartless woman of fashion—on these, and on a hundred more, he turns it, inexorably smiling, just at the compromising moment; then turns it off again, to leave us with a vision that we can never forget. Nor is it only by its vividness that his portraiture excels. At its best it rises into the region of sublimity, giving us new visions of the grandeur to which the human spirit can attain. It is sometimes said that the essence of Molière lies in his common sense; that his fundamental doctrine is the value of moderation, of the calm average outlook of the sensible man of the world—*l'honnête homme*. And no doubt this teaching is to be found throughout his work, devoted as it is, by its very nature, to the eccentricities and exaggerations which beset humanity. But if he had been nothing more than a sober propounder of the golden mean he never would have come to greatness. No man realized more clearly the importance of good sense; but he saw farther than that: he looked into the profundities of the soul, and measured those strange forces which brush aside the feeble dictates of human wisdom like gossamer, and lend, by their very lack of compromise, a dignity and almost a nobility to folly and even vice itself. Thus it is that he has invested the feeble, miserable Harpagon with a kind of sordid splendour, and that he has elevated the scoundrel Don Juan into an alarming image of intellectual power and pride. In his satire on learned ladies—*Les Femmes Savantes*—the ridicule is incessant, remorseless; the absurd, pedantic, self-complacent women are turned inside out before our eyes amid a cataract of laughter; and, if Molière had been merely the well-balanced moralist some critics suppose, that, no doubt, would have been enough. But for the true Molière it was not enough. The impression which he leaves upon us at the end of the play is not simply one of the utter folly of learning out of place; in Philaminte, the central female figure, he has depicted the elevation that belongs even to a mistaken and perverted love of what is excellent; and when she finally goes out, ridiculous, baffled, but as unyielding as ever in her devotion to grammar and astronomy, we come near, in the face of her majestic absurdity, to a feeling of respect. More remarkable still is Molière's portrayal of the eminence of the human spirit in the case of Tartufe. Here it is vice in its meanest and most repulsive forms which has become endowed with an awful grandeur. Tartufe, the hypocrite, the swindler, the seducer of his benefactor's wife, looms out on us with the kind of horrible greatness that Milton's Satan might have had if he had come to live with a bourgeois family in seventeenth-century France.

Molière's genius was many-sided; he was a master not only of the smile, but of the laugh. He is the gayest of writers, and his farces, in their wild hilarity, their contagious absurdity, are perfect models of what a farce should be. He has made these light, frivolous, happy things as eternal as the severest and the weightiest works of man. He has filled them with a wonderful irresponsible wisdom, condensing into single phrases the ridiculousness of generations: 'Nous avons changé tout cela.'—'Que diable allait-il faire dans cette galère?'—'Vous êtes orfèvre, Monsieur Josse.' So effectually has he contrived to embalm in the spice of his humour even the momentary affectations of his own time that they have come down to us fresh as when they first appeared, and the *Précieuses Ridicules*—a skit upon the manners and modes of speech affected by the fops of 1650—still raises to-day our inextinguishable laughter. This is the obvious side of Molière; and it is hardly in need of emphasis.

It is the more remote quality of his mind—his brooding melancholy, shot through with bitterness and doubt—that may at first sight escape the notice of the reader, and that will repay the deepest attention. His greatest works come near to tragedy. *Le Tartufe*, in spite of its patched-up happy ending, leaves an impression of horror upon the mind. *Don Juan* seems to inculcate a lesson of fatalistic scepticism. In this extraordinary play—of all Molière's works the farthest removed from the classical ideal—the conventional rules of religion and morality are exposed to a withering scorn; Don Juan, the very embodiment of the arrogance of intellect, and his servant Sganarelle, the futile and superstitious supporter of decency and law, come before us as the only alternatives for our choice; the antithesis is never resolved; and, though in the end the cynic is destroyed by a *coup de théâtre*, the fool in all his foolishness still confronts us when the curtain falls.

Don Juan—so enigmatic in its meaning and so loose in its structure—might almost be the work of some writer of the late nineteenth century; but *Le Misanthrope*—at once so harmonious and so brilliant, so lucid and so profound—could only have been produced in the age of Louis XIV. Here, in all probability, Molière's genius reached its height. The play shows us a small group of ladies and gentlemen, in the midst of which one man—Alceste—stands out pre-eminent for the intensity of his feelings and the honesty of his thoughts. He is in love with Célimène, a brilliant and fascinating woman of the world; and the subject of the play is his disillusionment. The plot is of the slightest; the incidents are very few. With marvellous art Molière brings on the inevitable disaster. Célimène will not give up the world for the sake of Alceste; and he will take her on no other terms. And that is all. Yet, when the play ends, how much has been revealed to us! The figure of Alceste has been often taken as a piece of self-portraiture; and indeed it is difficult not to believe that some at any rate of Molière's own characteristics have gone to the making of this subtle and sympathetic creation. The essence of Alceste is not his misanthropy (the title of the play is somewhat misleading), it is his sensitiveness. He alone, of all the characters in the piece, really feels intensely. He alone loves, suffers, and understands. His melancholy is the melancholy of a profound disillusionment. Molière, one fancies, might have looked out upon the world just so—from 'ce petit coin sombre, avec mon noir chagrin'. The world! To Alceste, at any rate, the world was the great enemy—a thing of vain ideals, cold hearts, and futile consolations. He pitted himself against it, and he failed. The world swept on remorselessly, and left him, in his little corner, alone. That was his tragedy. Was it Molière's also?—a tragedy, not of kings and empires, of vast catastrophes and magnificent imaginations; but something hardly less moving, and hardly less sublime—a tragedy of ordinary life.

Englishmen have always loved Molière. It is hardly an exaggeration to say that they have always detested RACINE. English critics, from Dryden to Matthew Arnold, have steadily refused to allow him a place among the great writers of the world; and the ordinary English reader of to-day probably thinks of him—if he thinks of him at all—as a dull, frigid, conventional writer, who went out of fashion with full-bottomed wigs and never wrote a line of true poetry. Yet in France Racine has been the object of almost universal admiration; his plays still hold the stage and draw forth the talents of the greatest actors; and there can be no doubt that it is the name of Racine that would first rise to the lips of an educated Frenchman if he were asked to select the one consummate master from among all the writers of his race. Now in literature, no less than in politics, you cannot indict a whole nation. Some justice, some meaning, France must have when she declares with one voice that Racine is not only one of the greatest of dramatists, but also one of the greatest of poets; and it behoves an Englishman, before he condemns or despises a foreign writer, to practise some humility and do his best to understand the point of view from which that writer is regarded by his own compatriots. No doubt, in the case of Racine, this is a particularly difficult matter. There are genuine national antipathies to be got over— real differences in habits of thought and of taste. But this very difficulty, when it is once surmounted, will make the gain the greater. For it will be a gain, not only in the appreciation of one additional artist, but in the appreciation of a new *kind* of artist; it will open up a whole undiscovered country in the continent of art.

English dramatic literature is, of course, dominated by Shakespeare; and it is almost inevitable that an English reader should measure the value of other poetic drama by the standards which Shakespeare has already implanted in his mind. But, after all, Shakespeare himself was but the product and the crown of a particular dramatic convention; he did not compose his plays according to an ideal pattern; he was an Elizabethan, working so consistently according to the methods of his age and country that, as we know, he passed 'unguessed at' among his contemporaries. But what were these methods and this convention? To judge of them properly we must look, not at Shakespeare's masterpieces, for they are transfused and consecrated with the light of transcendent genius, but at the average play of an ordinary Elizabethan play-wright, or even at one of the lesser works of Shakespeare himself. And, if we look here, it will become apparent that the dramatic tradition of the Elizabethan age was an extremely faulty one. It allowed, it is true, of great richness, great variety, and the sublimest heights of poetry; but it also allowed of an almost incredible looseness of structure and vagueness of purpose, of dullness, of insipidity, and of bad taste. The genius of the Elizabethans was astonishing, but it was genius struggling with difficulties which were well-nigh insuperable; and, as a matter of fact, in spite of their amazing poetic and dramatic powers, their work has vanished from the stage, and is to-day familiar to but a few of the lovers of English literature. Shakespeare alone was not subdued to what he worked in. His overwhelming genius harmonized and ennobled the discordant elements of the Elizabethan tradition, and invested them not only with immortality, but with immortality understood of the people. His greatest works will continue to be acted and applauded so long as there is a theatre in England. But even Shakespeare himself was not always successful. One has only to look at some of his secondary plays—at *Troilus and Cressida*, for instance, or *Timon of Athens*—to see at once how inveterate and malignant were the diseases to which the dramatic methods of the Elizabethans were a prey. Wisdom and poetry are intertwined with flatness and folly; splendid situations drift purposeless to impotent conclusions; brilliant psychology alternates with the grossest indecency and the feeblest puns. 'O matter and impertinency mixed!' one is inclined to exclaim at such a spectacle. And then one is blinded once more by the glamour of *Lear* and *Othello*; one forgets the defective system in the triumph of a few exceptions, and all plays seem intolerable unless they were written on the principle which produced *Pericles* and *Titus Andronicus* and the whole multitude of distorted and disordered works of genius of the Elizabethan age.

Racine's principles were, in fact, the direct opposite of these. 'Comprehension' might be taken as the watchword of the Elizabethans; Racine's was 'concentration'. His great aim was to produce, not an extraordinary nor a complex work of art, but a flawless one; he wished to be all matter and no impertinency. His conception of a drama was of something swift, simple, inevitable; an action taken at the crisis, with no redundancies however interesting, no complications however suggestive, no irrelevances however beautiful—but plain, intense, vigorous, and splendid with nothing but its own essential force. Nor can there be any doubt that Racine's view of what a drama should be has been justified by the subsequent history of the stage. The Elizabethan tradition has died out—or rather it has left the theatre, and become absorbed in the modern novel; and it is the drama of crisis—such as Racine conceived it—which is now the accepted model of what a stage-play should be. And, in this connexion, we may notice an old controversy, which still occasionally raises its head in the waste places of criticism—the question of the three unities. In this controversy both sides have been content to repeat arguments which are in reality irrelevant and futile. It is irrelevant to consider whether the unities were or were not prescribed by Aristotle; and it is futile to ask whether the sense of probability is or is not more shocked by the scenic representation of an action of thirty-six hours than by one of twenty-four. The value of the unities does not depend either upon their traditional authority or—to use the French expression—upon their *vraisemblance*. Their true importance lies simply in their being a powerful means towards concentration. Thus it is clear that in an absolute sense they are neither good nor bad; their goodness or badness depends upon the kind of result which the dramatist is aiming at. If he wishes to produce a drama of the Elizabethan type—a drama of comprehension—which shall include as much as possible of the varied manifestations of human life, then obviously the observance of the unities must exercise a restricting and narrowing influence which would be quite out of place. On the other hand, in a drama of crisis they are not only useful but almost inevitable. If a crisis is to be a real crisis it must not drag on indefinitely; it must not last for more than a few hours, or—to put a rough limit—for more than a single day; in fact, the unity of time must be preserved. Again, if the action is to pass quickly, it must pass in one place, for there will be no time for the movement of the characters elsewhere; thus the unity of place becomes a necessity. Finally, if the mind is to be concentrated to the full upon a particular crisis, it must not be distracted by side issues; the event, and nothing but the event, must be displayed; in other words, the dramatist will not succeed in his object unless he employs the unity of action.

Let us see how Racine carries out these principles by taking one of his most characteristic plays—*Bérénice*—and comparing it with an equally characteristic work of Shakespeare's—*Antony and Cleopatra*. The comparison is particularly interesting because the two dramas, while diametrically opposed in treatment, yet offer some curious parallels in the subjects with which they deal. Both are concerned with a pair of lovers placed in the highest position of splendour and power; in both the tragedy comes about through a fatal discordance between the claims of love and of the world; in both the action passes in the age of Roman greatness, and vast imperial issues are intertwined with individual destinies. Of Shakespeare's drama it is hardly necessary to speak. Nowhere else, perhaps, has that universal genius displayed more completely the extraordinary fertility of his mind. The play is crammed full and running over with the multifarious activities of human existence. 'What is there in the whole of life, in all the experience of the world,' one is inclined to ask after a perusal of it, 'that is not to be found somewhere or other among these amazing pages?' This tremendous effect has been produced, in the first place, by means of the immense variety of the characters; persons of every rank and every occupation—generals and waiting-women, princesses and pirates, diplomatists and peasants, eunuchs and emperors—all these we have, and a hundred more; and, of course, as the grand consummation of all, we have the dazzling complexity of Cleopatra. But this mass of character could never have been presented to us without a corresponding variety of incident; and, indeed, the tragedy is packed with an endless succession of incidents—battles, intrigues, marriages, divorces, treacheries, reconciliations, deaths. The complicated action stretches over a long period of time and over a huge tract of space. The scene constantly shifts from Alexandria to Rome, from Athens to Messina, from Pompey's galley to the plains of Actium. Some commentators have been puzzled by the multitude of these changes, and when, for a scene of a few moments, Shakespeare shows us a Roman army marching through Syria, they have been able to see in it nothing more than a wanton violation of the rule of the unity of place; they have not understood that it is precisely by such touches as these that Shakespeare has succeeded in bringing before our minds a sense of universal agitation and the enormous dissolution of empires.

Turning to *Bérénice*, we find a curious contrast. The whole tragedy takes place in a small antechamber; the action lasts hardly longer than its actual performance—about two hours and a half; and the characters are three in number. As for the plot, it is contained in the following six words of Suetonius: 'Titus reginam Berenicem dimissit invitus invitam.' It seems extraordinary that with such materials Racine should have ventured to set out to write a tragedy: it is more extraordinary still that he succeeded. The interest of the play never ceases for a moment; the simple situation is exposed, developed, and closed with all the refinements of art; nothing is omitted that is essential, nothing that is unessential is introduced. Racine has studiously avoided anything approaching violent action or contrast or complexity; he has relied entirely for his effect upon his treatment of a few intimate human feelings interacting among themselves. The strain and press of the outer world—that outer world which plays so great a part in Shakespeare's masterpiece—is almost banished from his drama—almost, but not quite. With wonderful art Racine manages to suggest that, behind the quiet personal crisis in the retired little room, the strain and the pressure of outside things do exist. For this is the force that separates the lovers—the cruel claims of government and the state. When, at the critical moment, Titus is at last obliged to make the fatal choice, one word, as he hesitates, seems to dominate and convince his soul: it is the word 'Rome'. Into this single syllable Racine has distilled his own poignant version of the long-resounding elaborations of *Antony and Cleopatra*.

It would, no doubt, be absurd to claim for Racine's tragedy a place as high as Shakespeare's. But this fact should not blind us to the extraordinary merits which it does possess. In one respect, indeed, it might be urged that the English play is surpassed by the French one—and that is, as a *play*. *Bérénice* is still acted with success; but *Antony and Cleopatra*—? It is impossible to do justice to such a work on the stage; it must be mutilated, rearranged, decocted, and in the end, at the best, it will hardly do more than produce an impression of confused splendour on an audience. It is the old difficulty of getting a quart into a pint bottle. But *Bérénice is* a pint—neither more nor less, and fits its bottle to a nicety. To witness a performance of it is a rare and exquisite pleasure; the impression is one of flawless beauty; one comes away profoundly moved, and with a new vision of the capacities of art.

Singleness of purpose is the dominating characteristic of the French classical drama, and of Racine's in particular; and this singleness shows itself not only in the action and its accessories, but in the whole tone of the piece. Unity of tone is, in fact, a more important element in a play than any other unity. To obtain it Racine and his school avoided both the extreme contrasts and the displays of physical action which the Elizabethans delighted in. The mixture of comedy and tragedy was abhorrent to Racine, not because it was bad in itself, but because it must have shattered the unity of his tone; and for the same reason he preferred not to produce before the audience the most exciting and disturbing circumstances of his plots, but to present them indirectly, by means of description. Now it is clear that the great danger lying before a dramatist who employs these methods is the danger of dullness. Unity of tone is an excellent thing, but if the tone is a tedious one, it is better to avoid it. Unfortunately Racine's successors in Classical Tragedy did not realize this truth. They did not understand the difficult art of keeping interest alive without variety of mood, and consequently their works are now almost unreadable. The truth is that they were deluded by the apparent ease with which Racine accomplished this difficult task. Having inherited his manner, they were content; they forgot that there was something else which they had not inherited—his genius.

Closely connected with this difficulty there was another over which Racine triumphed no less completely, and which proved equally fatal to his successors. Hitherto we have been discussing the purely dramatic aspect of classical tragedy; we must not forget that this drama was also literary. The problem that Racine had to solve was complicated by the fact that he was working, not only with a restricted dramatic system, but with a restricted language. His vocabulary was an incredibly small one—the smallest, beyond a doubt, that ever a great poet had to deal with. But that was not all: the machinery of his verse was hampered by a thousand traditional restraints; artificial rules of every kind hedged round his inspiration; if he were to soar at all, he must soar in shackles. Yet, even here, Racine succeeded: he *did* soar—though it is difficult at first for the English reader to believe it. And here precisely similar considerations apply, as in the case of Racine's dramatic method. In both instances the English reader is looking for variety, surprise, elaboration; and when he is given, instead, simplicity, clarity, ease, he is apt to see nothing but insipidity and flatness. Racine's poetry differs as much from Shakespeare's as some calm-flowing river of the plain from a turbulent mountain torrent. To the dwellers in the mountain the smooth river may seem at first unimpressive. But still waters run deep; and the proverb applies with peculiar truth to the poetry of Racine. Those ordinary words, that simple construction—what can there be there to deserve our admiration? On the surface, very little no doubt; but if we plunge below the surface we shall find a great profundity and a singular strength. Racine is in reality a writer of extreme force—but it is a force of absolute directness that he wields. He uses the commonest words, and phrases which are almost colloquial; but every word, every phrase, goes straight to its mark, and the impression produced is ineffaceable. In English literature there is very little of such writing. When an English poet wishes to be forceful he almost invariably flies to the gigantic, the unexpected, and the out-of-the-way; he searches for strange metaphors and extraordinary constructions; he surprises us with curious mysteries and imaginations we have never dreamed of before. Now and then, however, even in English literature, instances arise of the opposite—the Racinesque—method. In these lines of Wordsworth, for example—

> *The silence that is in the starry sky,*
> *The sleep that is among the lonely hills—*

there is no violent appeal, nothing surprising, nothing odd—only a direct and inevitable beauty; and such is the kind of effect which Racine is constantly producing. If he wishes to suggest the emptiness, the darkness, and the ominous hush of a night by the seashore, he does so not by strange similes or the accumulation of complicated details, but in a few ordinary, almost insignificant words—

Mais tout dort, et l'armée, et les vents, et Neptune.

If he wishes to bring before the mind the terrors of nightmare, a single phrase can conjure them up—

C'était pendant l'horreur d'une profonde nuit.

By the same simple methods his art can describe the wonderful and perfect beauty of innocence—

Le jour n'est pas plus pur que le fond de mon coeur;

and the furies of insensate passion—

C'est Vénus toute entière à sa proie attachée.

But the flavour of poetry vanishes in quotation—and particularly Racine's, which depends to an unusual extent on its dramatic surroundings, and on the atmosphere that it creates. He who wishes to appreciate it to the full must steep himself in it deep and long. He will be rewarded. In spite of a formal and unfamiliar style, in spite of a limited vocabulary, a conventional versification, an unvaried and uncoloured form of expression—in spite of all these things (one is almost inclined, under the spell of Racine's enchantment, to say *because* of them)—he will find a new beauty and a new splendour—a subtle and abiding grace.

But Racine's extraordinary powers as a writer become still more obvious when we consider that besides being a great poet he is also a great psychologist. The combination is extremely rare in literature, and in Racine's case it is especially remarkable owing to the smallness of the linguistic resources at his disposal and the rigid nature of the conventions in which he worked. That he should have succeeded in infusing into his tiny commonplace vocabulary, arranged in rhymed couplets according to the strictest and most artificial rules, not only the beauty of true poetry, but the varied subtleties of character and passion, is one of those miracles of art which defy analysis. Through the flowing regularity of his Alexandrines his personages stand out distinct and palpable, in all the vigour of life. The presentment, it is true, is not a detailed one; the accidents of character are not shown us—only its essentials; the human spirit comes before us shorn of its particulars, naked and intense. Nor is it—as might, perhaps, have been expected—in the portrayal of intellectual characters that Racine particularly excels; it is in the portrayal of passionate ones. His supreme mastery is over the human heart—the subtleties, the profundities, the agonies, the triumphs, of love. His gallery of lovers is a long one, and the greatest portraits in it are of women. There is the jealous, terrific Hermione; the delicate, melancholy Junie; the noble, exquisite, and fascinating Bérénice; there is Roxane with her voluptuous ruthlessness, and Monime with her purity and her courage; and there is the dark, incomparable splendour of Phèdre.

Perhaps the play in which Racine's wonderful discrimination in the drawing of passionate character may be seen in its most striking light is *Andromaque*. Here there are four characters—two men and two women—all under the dominion of intense feeling, and each absolutely distinct. Andromaque, the still youthful widow of Hector, cares for only two things in the world with passionate devotion—her young son Astyanax, and the memory of her husband. Both are the captives of Pyrrhus, the conqueror of Troy, a straightforward, chivalrous, but somewhat barbarous prince, who, though he is affianced to Hermione, is desperately in love with Andromaque. Hermione is a splendid tigress consumed by her desire for Pyrrhus; and Oreste is a melancholy, almost morbid man, whose passion for Hermione is the dominating principle of his life. These are the ingredients of the tragedy, ready to explode like gunpowder with the slightest spark. The spark is lighted when Pyrrhus declares to Andromaque that if she will not marry him he will execute her son. Andromaque consents, but decides secretly to kill herself immediately after the marriage, and thus ensure both the safety of Astyanax and the honour of Hector's wife. Hermione, in a fury of jealousy, declares that she will fly with Oreste, on one condition—that he kills Pyrrhus. Oreste, putting aside all considerations of honour and friendship, consents; he kills Pyrrhus, and then returns to his mistress to claim his reward. There follows one of the most violent scenes that Racine ever wrote—in which Hermione, in an agony of remorse and horror, turns upon her wretched lover and denounces his crime. Forgetful of her own instigation, she demands who it was that suggested to him the horrible deed—'*Qui te l'a dit?*' she shrieks: one of those astounding phrases which, once heard, can never be forgotten. She rushes out to commit suicide, and the play ends with Oreste mad upon the stage.

The appearance of this exciting and vital drama, written when Racine was twenty-eight years old, brought him immediate fame. During the next ten years (1667–77) he produced a series of masterpieces, of which perhaps the most interesting are *Britannicus*, where the youthful Nero, just plunging into crime, is delineated with supreme mastery; *Bajazet*, whose subject is a contemporary tragedy of the seraglio at Constantinople; and a witty comedy, *Les Plaideurs*, based on Aristophanes. Racine's character was a complex one; he was at once a brilliant and caustic man of the world, a profound scholar, a sensitive and emotional poet. He was extremely combative, quarrelling both with the veteran Corneille and with the friend who had first helped him towards success—Molière; and he gave vent to his antipathies in some very vigorous and cutting prose prefaces as well as in some verse epigrams which are among the most venomous in the language. Besides this, he was an assiduous courtier, and he also found the time, among these various avocations, for carrying on at least two passionate love-affairs. At the age of thirty-eight, after two years' labour, he completed the work in which his genius shows itself in its consummate form—the great tragedy of *Phèdre*. The play contains one of the most finished and beautiful, and at the same time one of the most overwhelming studies of passion in the literature of the world. The tremendous rôle of Phèdre—which, as the final touchstone of great acting, holds the same place on the French stage as that of Hamlet on the English—dominates the piece, rising in intensity as act follows act, and 'horror on horror's head accumulates'. Here, too, Racine has poured out all the wealth of his poetic powers. He has performed the last miracle, and infused into the ordered ease of the Alexandrine a strange sense of brooding mystery and indefinable terror and the awful approaches of fate. The splendour of the verse reaches its height in the fourth act, when the ruined queen, at the culmination of her passion, her remorse, and her despair, sees in a vision Hell opening to receive her, and the appalling shade of her father Minos dispensing his unutterable doom. The creator of this magnificent passage, in which the imaginative grandeur of the loftiest poetry and the supreme force of dramatic emotion are mingled in a perfect whole, has a right to walk beside Sophocles in the high places of eternity.

Owing to the intrigues of a lady of fashion, *Phèdre*, when it first appeared, was a complete failure. An extraordinary change then took place in Racine's mind. A revulsion of feeling, the precise causes of which are to this day a mystery, led him suddenly to renounce the world, to retire into the solitude of religious meditation, and to abandon the art which he had practised with such success. He was not yet forty, his genius was apparently still developing, but his great career was at an end. Towards the close of his life he produced two more plays—*Esther*, a short idyllic piece of great beauty, and *Athalie*, a tragedy which, so far from showing that his powers had declined during his long retreat, has been pronounced by some critics to be the finest of his works. He wrote no more for the stage, and he died eight years later, at the age of sixty. It is difficult to imagine the loss sustained by literature during those twenty years of silence. They might have given us a dozen tragedies, approaching, or even surpassing, the merit of *Phèdre*. And Racine must have known this. One is tempted to see in his mysterious mortification an instance of that strain of disillusionment which runs like a dark thread through the brilliant texture of the literature of the *Grand Siècle*. Racine had known to the full the uses of this world, and he had found them flat, stale, and unprofitable; he had found that even the triumphs of his art were all compact of worldliness; and he had turned away, in an agony of renunciation, to lose himself in the vision of the Saints.

The influence and the character of that remarkable age appear nowhere more clearly than in the case of its other great poet—LA FONTAINE. In the Middle Ages, La Fontaine would have been a mendicant friar, or a sainted hermit, or a monk, surreptitiously illuminating the margins of his manuscripts with the images of birds and beasts. In the nineteenth century, one can imagine him drifting among Paris cafés, pouring out his soul in a random lyric or two, and dying before his time. The age of Louis XIV took this dreamer, this idler, this feckless, fugitive, spiritual creature, kept him alive by means of patrons in high society, and eventually turned him—not simply into a poet, for he was a poet by nature, but into one of the most subtle, deliberate, patient, and exquisite craftsmen who have ever written in verse. The process was a long one; La Fontaine was in his fifties when he wrote the greater number of his *Fables*—where his genius found its true expression for the first time. But the process was also complete. Among all the wonderful and beautiful examples of masterly craftsmanship in the poetry of France, the *Fables* of La Fontaine stand out as *the* models of what perfect art should be.

The main conception of the fables was based upon the combination of two ideas—that of the stiff dry moral apologue of Æsop, and that of the short story. By far the most important of these two elements was the latter. With the old fabulists the moral was the excuse for the fable; with La Fontaine it was the other way round. His moral, added in a conventional tag, or even, sometimes, omitted altogether, was simply of use as the point of departure for the telling of a charming little tale. Besides this, the traditional employment of animals as the personages in a fable served La Fontaine's turn in another way. It gave him the opportunity of creating a new and delightful atmosphere, in which his wit, his fancy, his humour, and his observation could play at their ease. His animals—whatever injudicious enthusiasts may have said—are not real animals; we are no wiser as to the true nature of cats and mice, foxes and lions, after we have read the *Fables* than before. Nor, on the other hand, are they the mere pegs for human attributes which they were in the hands of Æsop. La Fontaine's creatures partake both of the nature of real animals and of human beings, and it is precisely in this dual character of theirs that their fascination lies. In their outward appearance they are deliciously true to life. With the fewest of rapid strokes, La Fontaine can raise up an unmistakable vision of any beast or bird, fish or reptile, that he has a mind to—

> *Un jour sur ses long pieds allait je ne sais où*
> *Le héron au long bec emmanché d'un long cou.*

Could there be a better description? And his fables are crowded with these life-like little vignettes. But the moment one goes below the surface one finds the frailties, the follies, the virtues and the vices of humanity. And yet it is not quite that. The creatures of La Fontaine's fantasy are not simply animals with the minds of human beings: they are something more complicated and amusing; they are animals with the minds which human beings would certainly have, if one could suppose them transformed into animals. When the young and foolish rat sees a cat for the first time and observes to his mother—

Je le crois fort sympathisant
Avec messieurs les rats: car il a des oreilles
En figure aux nôtres pareilles;

this excellent reason is obviously not a rat's reason; nor is it a human being's reason; the fun lies in its being just the reason which, no doubt, a silly young creature of the human species would give in the circumstances if, somehow or other, he were metamorphosed into a rat.

It is this world of shifting lights, of queer, elusive, delightful absurdities, that La Fontaine has made the scene of the greater number of his stories. The stories themselves are for the most part exceedingly slight; what gives them immortality is the way they are told. Under the guise of an ingenuous, old-world manner, La Fontaine makes use of an immense range of technical powers. He was an absolute master of the resources of metre; and his rhythms, far looser and more varied than those of his contemporaries, are marvellously expressive, while yet they never depart from a secret and controlling sense of form. His vocabulary is very rich—stocked chiefly with old-fashioned words, racy, colloquial, smacking of the soil, and put together with the light elliptical constructions of the common people. Nicknames he is particularly fond of: the cat is Raminagrobis, or Grippeminaud, or Rodilard, or Maître Mitis; the mice are 'la gent trotte-menu'; the stomach is Messer Gaster; Jupiter is Jupin; La Fontaine himself is Gros-Jean. The charming tales, one feels, might almost have been told by some old country crony by the fire, while the wind was whistling in the chimney and the winter night drew on. The smile, the gesture, the singular *naïveté*—one can watch it all. But only for a moment. One must be childish indeed (and, by an odd irony, this exquisitively sophisticated author falls into the hands of most of his readers when they are children) to believe, for more than a moment, that the ingenuousness of the *Fables* was anything but assumed. In fact, to do so would be to miss the real taste of the work. There is a kind of art, as every one knows, that conceals itself; but there is another—and this is less often recognized—that displays itself, that *just* shows, charmingly but unmistakably, how beautifully contrived it is. And La Fontaine's art is of the latter sort. He is like one of those accomplished cooks in whose dishes, though the actual secret of their making remains a mystery, one can trace the ingredients which have gone to the concoction of the delicious whole. As one swallows the rare morsel, one can just perceive how, behind the scenes, the oil, the vinegar, the olive, the sprinkling of salt, the drop of lemon were successively added, and, at the critical moment, the simmering delicacy served up, done to a turn.

It is indeed by an infinity of small touches that La Fontaine produces his effects. And his effects are very various. With equal ease, apparently, he can be playful, tender, serious, preposterous, eloquent, meditative, and absurd. But one quality is always present in his work; whatever tune he may be playing, there is never a note too much. Alike in his shortest six-lined anecdote and his most elaborate pieces, in which detail follows detail and complex scenes are developed, there is no trace of the superfluous; every word has its purpose in the general scheme. This quality appears most clearly, perhaps, in the adroit swiftness of his conclusions. When once the careful preliminary foundation of the story has been laid, the crisis comes quick and pointed—often in a single line. Thus we are given a minute description of the friendship of the cat and the sparrow; all sorts of details are insisted on; we are told how, when the sparrow teased the cat—

En sage et discrète personne,
Maître chat excusait ces jeux.

Then the second sparrow is introduced and his quarrel with the first. The cat fires up—

Le moineau du voisin viendra manger le nôtre?
Non, de par tous les chats!—Entrant lors au combat,
Il croque l'étranger. Vraiment, dit maître chat,
Les moineaux ont un gout exquis et délicat!

And now in one line the story ends—

Cette réflexion fit aussi croquer l'autre.

One more instance of La Fontaine's inimitable conciseness may be given. When Bertrand (the monkey) has eaten the chestnuts which Raton (the cat) has pulled out of the fire, the friends are interrupted; the fable ends thus—

> *Une servante vint; adieu, mes gens! Raton*
> *N'était pas content, ce dit-on.*

How admirable are the brevity and the lightness of that 'adieu, mes gens'! In three words the instantaneous vanishing of the animals is indicated with masterly precision. One can almost see their tails whisking round the corner.

Modern admirers of La Fontaine have tended to throw a veil of sentiment over his figure, picturing him as the consoling beatific child of nature, driven by an unsympathetic generation to a wistful companionship with the dumb world of brutes. But nothing could be farther from the truth than this conception. La Fontaine was as unsentimental as Molière himself. This does not imply that he was unfeeling: feelings he had—delicate and poignant ones; but they never dominated him to the exclusion of good sense. His philosophy—if we may call so airy a thing by such a name—was the philosophy of some gentle whimsical follower of Epicurus. He loved nature, but unromantically, as he loved a glass of wine and an ode of Horace, and the rest of the good things of life. As for the bad things—they were there; he saw them—saw the cruelty of the wolf, and the tyranny of the lion, and the rapacity of man—saw that—

> *Jupin pour chaque état mit deux tables au monde;*
> *L'adroit, le vigilant, et le fort sont assis*
> *A la première; et les petits*
> *Mangent leur reste à la seconde.*

Yet, while he saw them, he could smile. It was better to smile—if only with regret; better, above all, to pass lightly, swiftly, gaily over the depths as well as the surface of existence; for life is short—almost as short as one of his own fables—

> *Qui de nous des clartés de la voûte azurée*
> *Doit jouir le dernier? Est-il aucun moment*
> *Qui vous puisse assurer d'un second seulement?*

The age was great in prose as well as in poetry. The periods of BOSSUET, ordered, lucid, magnificent, reflect its literary ideals as clearly as the couplets of Racine. Unfortunately, however, in the case of Bossuet, the splendour and perfection of the form is very nearly all that a modern reader can appreciate: the substance is for the most part uninteresting and out-of-date. The truth is that Bossuet was too completely a man of his own epoch to speak with any great significance to after generations. His melodious voice enters our ears, but not our hearts. The honest, high-minded, laborious bishop, with his dignity and his enthusiasm, his eloquence and his knowledge of the world, represents for us the best and most serious elements in the Court of Louis. The average good man of those days must have thought on most subjects as Bossuet thought—though less finely and intensely; and Bossuet never spoke a sentence from his pulpit which went beyond the mental vision of the most ordinary of his congregation. He saw all round his age, but he did not see beyond it. Thus, in spite of his intelligence, his view of the world was limited. The order of things under Louis XIV was the one order: outside that, all was confusion, heresy, and the work of Satan. If he had written more often on the great unchanging fundamentals of life, more of his work would have been enduring. But it happened that, while by birth he was an artist, by profession he was a theologian; and even the style of Bossuet can hardly save from oblivion the theological controversies of two hundred years ago. The same failing mars his treatment of history. His *Histoire Universelle* was conceived on broad and sweeping lines, and contains some perspicacious thinking; but the dominating notion of the book is a theological one—the illustration, by means of the events of history, of the divine governance of the world; and the fact that this conception of history has now become extinct has reduced the work to the level of a finely written curiosity.

Purely as a master of prose Bossuet stands in the first rank. His style is broad, massive, and luminous; and the great bulk of his writing is remarkable more for its measured strength than for its ornament. Yet at times the warm spirit of the artist, glowing through the well-ordered phrases, diffuses an extraordinary splendour. When, in his *Méditations sur l'Evangile* or his *Elévations sur les Mystères*, Bossuet unrolls the narratives of the Bible or meditates upon the mysteries of his religion, his language takes on the colours of poetry and soars on the steady wings of an exalted imagination. In his famous *Oraisons Funèbres* the magnificent amplitude of his art finds its full expression. Death, and Life, and the majesty of God, and the transitoriness of human glory—upon such themes he speaks with an organ-voice which reminds an English reader of the greatest of his English contemporaries, Milton. The pompous, rolling, resounding sentences follow one another in a long solemnity, borne forward by a vast movement of eloquence which underlies, controls, and animates them all.

> O nuit désastreuse! O nuit effroyable, où retentit tout-à-coup comme un éclat de tonnerre, cette étonnante nouvelle: Madame se meurt, Madame est morte! . . .

—The splendid words flow out like a stream of lava, molten and glowing, and then fix themselves for ever in adamantine beauty.

We have already seen that one of the chief characteristics of French classicism was compactness. The tragedies of Racine are as closely knit as some lithe naked runner without an ounce of redundant flesh; the *Fables* of La Fontaine are airy miracles of compression. In prose the same tendency is manifest, but to an even more marked degree. La Rochefoucauld and La Bruyère, writing the one at the beginning, the other towards the close, of the classical period, both practised the art of extreme brevity with astonishing success. The Duc De La Rochefoucauld was the first French writer to understand completely the wonderful capacities for epigrammatic statement which his language possessed; and in the dexterous precision of pointed phrase no succeeding author has ever surpassed him. His little book of *Maxims* consists of about five hundred detached sentences, polished like jewels, and, like jewels, sparkling with an inner brilliance on which it seems impossible that one can gaze too long. The book was the work of years, and it contains in its small compass the observations of a lifetime. Though the reflections are not formally connected, a common spirit runs through them all. 'Vanity of vanities! All is vanity!' such is the perpetual burden of La Rochefoucauld's doctrine: but it is vanity, not in the generalized sense of the Preacher, but in the ordinary personal sense of empty egotism and petty self-love which, in the eyes of this bitter moralist, is the ultimate essence of the human spirit and the secret spring of the world. The case is overstated, no doubt; but the strength of La Rochefoucauld's position can only be appreciated when one has felt for oneself the keen arrows of his wit. As one turns over his pages, the sentences strike into one with a deadly force of personal application; sometimes one almost blushes; one realizes that these things are cruel, that they are humiliating, and that they are true. 'Nous avons tous assez de force pour supporter les maux d'autrui.'—'Quelque bien qu'on nous dise de nous, on ne nous apprend rien de nouveau.'—'On croit quelquefois haïr la flatterie, mais on ne hait que le manière de flatter.'—'Le refus de la louange est un désir d'être loué deux fois.'—'Les passions les plus violentes nous laissent quelquefois du relâche, mais la vanité nous agite toujours.' No more powerful dissolvent for the self-complacency of humanity was ever composed.

Unlike the majority of the writers of his age, La Rochefoucauld was an aristocrat; and this fact gives a peculiar tone to his work. In spite of the great labour which he spent upon perfecting it, he has managed, in some subtle way, to preserve all through it an air of slight disdain. 'Yes, these sentences are all perfect,' he seems to be saying; 'but then, what else would you have? Unless one writes perfect sentences, why should one trouble to write?' In his opinion, 'le vrai honnête homme est celui qui ne se pique de rien'; and it is clear that he followed his own dictum. His attitude was eminently detached. Though what he says reveals so intensely personal a vision, he himself somehow remains impersonal. Beneath the flawless surface of his workmanship, the clever Duke eludes us. We can only see, as we peer into the recesses, an infinite ingenuity and a very bitter love of truth.

A richer art and a broader outlook upon life meet us in the pages of LA BRUYÈRE. The instrument is still the same—the witty and searching epigram—but it is no longer being played upon a single string. La Bruyère's style is extremely supple; he throws his apothegms into an infinite variety of moulds, employing a wide and coloured vocabulary, and a complete mastery of the art of rhetorical effect. Among these short reflections he has scattered a great number of somewhat lengthier portraits or character-studies, some altogether imaginary, others founded wholly or in part on well-known persons of the day. It is here that the great qualities of his style show themselves most clearly. Psychologically, these studies are perhaps less valuable than has sometimes been supposed: they are caricatures rather than portraits—records of the idiosyncrasies of humanity rather than of humanity itself. What cannot be doubted for a moment is the supreme art with which they have been composed. The virtuosity of the language—so solid and yet so brilliant, so varied and yet so pure—reminds one of the hard subtlety of a Greek gem. The rhythm is absolutely perfect, and, with its suspensions, its elaborations, its gradual crescendos, its unerring conclusions, seems to carry the sheer beauty of expressiveness to the farthest conceivable point. Take, as one instance out of a multitude, this description of the crank who devotes his existence to the production of tulips—

Vous le voyez planté et qui a pris racine au milieu de ses tulipes et devant la *Solitaire*: il ouvre de grands yeux, il frotte ses mains, il se baisse, il la voit de plus près, il ne l'a jamais vue si belle, il a le coeur épanoui de joie: il la quitte pour l'*Orientale*; de là, il va à la *Veuve*; il passe au *Drap d'or*, de celle-ci à *l'Agathe*, d'où il revient enfin à la *Solitaire*, où il se fixe, où il se lasse, où il s'assied, où il oublie de dîner: aussi est-elle nuancée, bordée, huilée a pièces emportées; elle a un beau vase ou un beau calice; il la contemple, il l'admire; Dieu et la nature sont en tout cela ce qu'il n'admire point! il ne va pas plus loin que l'oignon de sa tulipe, qu'il ne livrerait pas pour mille écus, et qu'il donnera pour rien quand les tulipes seront néligées et que les oeillets auront prévalu. Cet homme raisonnable qui a une âme, qui a un culte et une religion, revient chez soi fatigué affamé, mais fort content de sa journée: il a vu des tulipes.

Les Caractères is the title of La Bruyère's book; but its sub-title—'Les Moeurs de ce Siècle'—gives a juster notion of its contents. The whole of society, as it appeared to the subtle and penetrating gaze of La Bruyère, flows through its pages. In them, Versailles rises before us, less in its outward form than in its spiritual content—its secret, essential self. And the judgement which La Bruyère passes on this vision is one of withering scorn. His criticism is more convincing than La Rochefoucauld's because it is based upon a wider and a deeper foundation. The vanity which *he* saw around him was indeed the vanity of the Preacher—the emptiness, the insignificance, the unprofitableness, of worldly things. There was nothing too small to escape his terrible attention, and nothing too large. His arraignment passes from the use of rouge to the use of torture, from the hypocrisies of false devotion to the silly absurdities of eccentrics, from the inhumanity of princes to the little habits of fools. The passage in which he describes the celebration of Mass in the Chapel of Versailles, where all the courtiers were to be seen turning their faces to the king's throne and their backs to the altar of God, shows a spirit different indeed from that of Bossuet—a spirit not far removed from the undermining criticism of the eighteenth century itself. Yet La Bruyère was not a social reformer nor a political theorist: he was simply a moralist and an observer. He saw in a flash the condition of the French peasants—

Certains animaux farouches, des mâles et des femelles, répandus par la campagne, noirs, livides, et tout brulés du soleil, attachés à la terre qu'ils fouillent et qu'ils remuent avec une opiniâtreté invincible; ils out comme une voix articulée, et, quand ils se lèvent sur leurs pieds, ils montrent une face humaine: et en effet ils sont des hommes—

saw the dreadful fact, noted it with all the intensity of his genius, and then passed on. He was not concerned with finding remedies for the evils of a particular society, but with exposing the underlying evils of all societies. He would have written as truthful and as melancholy a book if he had lived to-day.

La Bruyère, in the darkness of his pessimism, sometimes suggests Swift, especially in his sarcastically serious treatment of detail; but he was without the virulent bitterness of the great Dean. In fact his indictment owes much of its impressiveness to the sobriety with which it is presented. There is no rage, no strain, no over-emphasis; one feels as one reads that this is an impartial judge. And, more than that, one feels that the judge is not only a judge, but also a human being. It is the human quality in La Bruyère's mind which gives his book its rare flavour, so that one seems to hear, in these printed words, across the lapse of centuries, the voice of a friend. At times he forgets his gloom and his misanthropy, and speaks with a strange depth of feeling on friendship or on love. 'Un beau visage,' he murmurs, 'est le plus beau de tous les spectacles, et l'harmonie la plus douce est le son de voix de celle que l'on aime.' And then—'Être avec les gens qu'on aime, cela suffit; rever, leur parler, ne leur parler point, penser à eux, penser à des choses plus indifférentes, mais auprès d'eux tout est égal.' How tender and moving the accent, yet how restrained? And was ever more profundity of intimacy distilled into a few simple words than here—'Il y a du plaisir à rencontrer les yeux de celui à qui l'on vient de donner'? But then once more the old melancholy seizes him. Even love itself must end.—'On guérit comme on se console; on n'a pas dans le coeur de quoi toujours pleurer et toujours aimer.' He is overwhelmed by the disappointments of life.—'Les choses les plus souhaitées n'arrivent point; ou, si elles arrivent, ce n'est ni dans le temps ni dans les circonstances où elles auraient fait un extrême plaisir.' And life itself, what is it? how does it pass?—'Il n'y a pour l'homme que trois événements: naître, vivre, et mourir; il ne se sent pas naître, il souffre à mourir, et il oublie de vivre.'

The pages of La Bruyère—so brilliant and animated on the surface, so sombre in their fundamental sense—contain the final summary—we might almost say the epitaph—of the great age of Louis XIV. Within a few years of the publication of his book in its complete form (1694), the epoch, which had begun in such a blaze of splendour a generation earlier, entered upon its ultimate phase of disaster and humiliation. The political ambitions of the overweening king were completely shattered; the genius of Marlborough annihilated the armies of France; and when peace came at last it came in ruin. The country was not only exhausted to the farthest possible point, its recuperation had been made well-nigh impossible by the fatal Revocation of the Edict of Nantes, which, in circumstances of the utmost cruelty, had driven into exile the most industrious and independent portion of the population. Poverty, discontent, tyranny, fanaticism—such was the legacy that Louis left to his country. Yet that was not quite all. Though, during the last years of the reign, French literature achieved little of lasting value, the triumphs of the earlier period threw a new and glorious lustre over the reputation of France. The French tongue became the language of culture throughout Europe. In every department of literature, French models and French taste were regarded as the supreme authorities. Strange as it would have seemed to him, it was not as the conqueror of Holland nor as the defender of the Church, but as the patron of Racine and the protector of Molière that the superb and brilliant Louis gained his highest fame, his true immortality.

V

The Eighteenth Century

The eighteenth century in France began with Louis XIV and ended with the Revolution. It is the period which bridges the gulf between autocracy and self-government, between Roman Catholicism and toleration, between the classical spirit and the spirit of the Romantic Revival. It is thus of immense importance in the history not only of France, but of the civilized world. And from the point of view of literature it is also peculiarly interesting. The vast political and social changes which it inaugurated were the result of a corresponding movement in the current of ideas; and this movement was begun, developed, and brought to a triumphant conclusion by a series of great French writers, who deliberately put their literary abilities to the service of the causes which they had at heart. Thus the literature of the epoch offers a singular contrast to that of the preceding one. While the masterpieces of the *Grand Siècle* served no ulterior purpose, coming into being and into immortality simply as works of beauty and art, those of the eighteenth century were works of propaganda, appealing with a practical purpose to the age in which they were written—works whose value does not depend solely upon artistic considerations. The former were static, the latter dynamic. As the century progressed, the tendency deepened; and the literature of the age, taken as a whole, presents a spectacle of thrilling dramatic interest, in which the forces of change, at first insignificant, gradually gather in volume, and at last, accumulated into overwhelming power, carry all before them. In pure literature, the writers of the eighteenth century achieved, indeed, many triumphs; but their great, their peculiar, triumphs were in the domain of thought.

The movement had already begun before the death of Louis. The evils at which La Bruyère had shuddered had filled the attention of more practical minds. Among these the most remarkable was FÉNELON, Archbishop of Cambray, who combined great boldness of political thought with the graces of a charming and pellucid style. In several writings, among which was the famous *Télémaque*—a book written for the edification of the young Duc de Bourgogne, the heir to the French throne—Fénelon gave expression to the growing reaction against the rigid autocracy of the government, and enunciated the revolutionary doctrine that a monarch existed for no other purpose than the good of his people. The Duc de Bourgogne was converted to the mild, beneficent, and open-minded views of his tutor; and it is possible that if he had lived a series of judicious reforms might have prevented the cataclysm at the close of the century. But in one important respect the mind of Fénelon was not in accord with the lines on which French thought was to develop for the next eighty years. Though he was among the first to advocate religious toleration, he was an ardent, even a mystical, Roman Catholic. Now one of the chief characteristics of the coming age was its scepticism—its elevation of the secular as opposed to the religious elements in society, and its utter lack of sympathy with all forms of mystical devotion. Signs of this spirit also had appeared before the end of Louis's reign. As early as 1687—within a year of the Revocation of the Edict of Nantes—FONTENELLE, the nephew of Corneille, in his *Histoire des Oracles*, attacked the miraculous basis of Christianity under the pretence of exposing the religious credulity of the ancient Greeks and Romans. In its mingling of the sprightly and the erudite, and in the subdued irony of its apparent submission to orthodoxy, this little book forestalled a method of controversy which came into great vogue at a later date. But a more important work, published at the very end of the seventeenth century, was the *Dictionary* of BAYLE, in which, amid an enormous mass of learning poured out over a multitude of heterogeneous subjects, the most absolute religious scepticism is expressed with unmistakable emphasis and unceasing reiteration. The book is an extremely unwieldy one—very large and very discursive, and quite devoid of style; but its influence was immense; and during the long combat of the eighteenth century it was used as a kind of armoury, supplying many of their sharpest weapons to the writers of the time.

It was not, however, until a few years after the death of the great king that a volume appeared which contained a complete expression of the new spirit, in all its aspects. In the *Lettres Persanes* of MONTESQUIEU (published 1721) may be discerned the germs of the whole thought of the eighteenth century in France. The scheme of this charming and remarkable book was not original: some Eastern travellers were supposed to arrive in Paris, and to describe, in a correspondence with their countrymen in Persia, the principal features of life in the French capital. But the uses to which Montesquieu put this borrowed plot were all his own. He made it the base for a searching attack on the whole system of the government of Louis XIV. The corruption of the Court, the privileges of the nobles, the maladministration of the finances, the stupidities and barbarisms of the old autocratic régime—these are the topics to which he is perpetually drawing his reader's attention. But he does more than this: his criticism is not merely particular, it is general; he points out the necessarily fatal effects of all despotisms, and he indicates his own conception of what a good constitution should be. All these discussions are animated by a purely secular spirit. He views religion from an outside standpoint; he regards it rather as one of the functions of administration than as an inner spiritual force. As for all the varieties of fanaticism and intolerance, he abhors them utterly.

It might be supposed that a book containing such original and far-reaching theories was a solid substantial volume, hard to master and laborious to read. The precise opposite is the case. Montesquieu has dished up his serious doctrines into a spicy story, full of epigrams and light topical allusions, and romantic adventures, and fancy visions of the East. Montesquieu was a magistrate; yet he ventured to indulge here and there in reflections of dubious propriety, and to throw over the whole of his book an airy veil of voluptuous intrigue. All this is highly typical of the literature of the age which was now beginning. The serious, formal tone of the classical writers was abandoned, and was replaced by a gay, unemphatic, pithy manner, in which some grains of light-hearted licentiousness usually gave a flavour to the wit. The change was partly due to the shifting of the centre of society from the elaborate and spectacular world of Versailles to the more intimate atmosphere of the drawing-rooms of Paris. With the death of the old king the ceremonial life of the Court fell into the background; and the spirits of the time flew off into frivolity with a sense of freedom and relief. But there was another influence at work. Paradoxical as it may sound, it was the very seriousness of the new writers which was the real cause of their lack of decorum. Their great object was to be read—and by the largest possible number of readers; the old select circle of literary connoisseurs no longer satisfied them; they were eager to preach their doctrines to a wider public—to the brilliant, inquisitive, and increasingly powerful public of the capital. And with this public no book had a chance of success unless it was of the kind that could be run through rapidly, pleasantly, on a sofa, between dinner and the opera, and would furnish the material for spicy anecdotes and good talk. Like the jesters of the Middle Ages, the philosophers of the eighteenth century found in the use of pranks and buffoonery the best way of telling the truth.

Until about the middle of the century, Montesquieu was the dominating figure in French thought. His second book—*Considérations sur la Grandeur et la Décadence des Romains*—is an exceedingly able work, in which a series of interesting and occasionally profound historical reflections are expressed in a style of great brilliance and incisiveness. Here Montesquieu definitely freed history from the medieval fetters which it had worn even in the days of Bossuet, and considered the development of events from a purely secular point of view, as the result of natural causes. But his greatest work, over which he spent the greater part of his life, and on which his reputation must finally rest, was *L'Esprit des Lois* (published in 1748). The discussion of this celebrated book falls outside the domain of literature, and belongs rather to the history of political thought. It is enough to say that here all Montesquieu's qualities—his power of generalization, his freedom from prejudice, his rationalism, his love of liberty and hatred of fanaticism, his pointed, epigrammatic style—appear in their most characteristic form. Perhaps the chief fault of the book is that it is too brilliant. When Madame du Deffand said that its title should have been *De l'Esprit sur les Lois* she put her finger on its weak spot. Montesquieu's generalizations are always bold, always original, always fine; unfortunately, they are too often unsound into the bargain. The fluid elusive facts slip through his neat sentences like water in a sieve. His treatment of the English constitution affords an illustration of this. One of the first foreigners to recognize the importance and to study the nature of English institutions, Montesquieu nevertheless failed to give an accurate account of them. He believed that he had found in them a signal instance of his favourite theory of the beneficial effects produced by the separation of the three powers of government—the judicial, the legislative, and the executive; but he was wrong. In England, as a matter of fact, the powers of the legislative and the executive were intertwined. This particular error has had a curious history. Montesquieu's great reputation led to his view of the constitution of England being widely accepted as the true one; as such it was adopted by the American leaders after the War of Independence; and its influence is plainly visible in the present constitution of the United States. Such is the strange power of good writing over the affairs of men!

At about the same time as the publication of the *Lettres Persanes*, there appeared upon the scene in Paris a young man whose reputation was eventually destined far to outshine that of Montesquieu himself. This young man was François Arouet, known to the world as Voltaire. Curiously enough, however, the work upon which Voltaire's reputation was originally built up has now sunk into almost complete oblivion. It was as a poet, and particularly as a tragic poet, that he won his fame; and it was primarily as a poet that he continued to be known to his contemporaries during the first sixty years of his life (1694–1754). But to-day his poetry—the serious part of it, at least,—is never read, and his tragedies—except for an occasional revival—are never acted. As a dramatist Voltaire is negligible for the very reasons that made him so successful in his own day. It was not his object to write great drama, but to please his audience: he did please them; and, naturally enough, he has not pleased posterity. His plays are melodramas—the melodramas of a very clever man with a great command of language, an acute eye for stage-effect, and a consummate knowledge of the situations and sentiments which would go down with his Parisian public. They are especially remarkable for their wretched psychology. It seems well-nigh incredible that Voltaire's pasteboard imitations of humanity should ever have held a place side by side with the profound presentments of Racine; yet so it was, and Voltaire was acclaimed as the equal—or possibly the triumphant rival—of his predecessor. All through the eighteenth century this singular absence of psychological insight may be observed.

The verse of the plays is hardly better than the character-drawing. It is sometimes good rhetoric; it is never poetry. The same may be said of *La Henriade*, the National Epic which placed Voltaire, in the eyes of his admiring countrymen, far above Milton and Dante, and, at least, on a level with Virgil and Homer. The true gifts displayed in this unreadable work were not poetical at all, but historical. The notes and dissertations appended to it showed that Voltaire possessed a real grasp of the principles of historical method—principles which he put to a better use a few years later in his brilliant narrative, based on original research, of the life of Charles XII.

During this earlier period of his activity Voltaire seems to have been trying—half unconsciously, perhaps—to discover and to express the fundamental quality of his genius. What was that quality? Was he first and foremost a dramatist, or an epic poet, or a writer of light verse, or an historian, or even perhaps a novelist? In all these directions he was working successfully—yet without absolute success. For, in fact, at bottom, he was none of these things: the true nature of his spirit was not revealed in them. When the revelation did come, it came as the result of an accident. At the age of thirty he was obliged, owing to a quarrel with a powerful nobleman, to leave France and take up his residence in England. The three years that he passed there had an immense effect upon his life. In those days England was very little known to Frenchmen; the barrier which had arisen during the long war between the two peoples was only just beginning to be broken down; and when Voltaire arrived, it was almost in the spirit of a discoverer. What he found filled him with astonishment and admiration. Here, in every department of life, were to be seen all the blessings so conspicuously absent in France. Here were wealth, prosperity, a contented people, a cultivated nobility, a mild and just administration, and a bursting energy which manifested itself in a multitude of ways—in literature, in commerce, in politics, in scientific thought. And all this had come into existence in a nation which had curbed the power of the monarchy, done away with priestcraft, established the liberty of the Press, set its face against every kind of bigotry and narrow-mindedness, and, through the means of free institutions, taken up the task of governing itself. The inference was obvious: in France also, like causes would lead to like results. When he was allowed to return to his own country, Voltaire published the outcome of his observations and reflections in his *Lettres Philosophiques*, where for the first time his genius displayed itself in its essential form. The book contains an account of England as Voltaire saw it, from the social rather than from the political point of view. English life is described in its actuality, detailed, vivid, and various; we are shown Quakers and members of Parliament, merchants and philosophers; we come in for the burial of Sir Isaac Newton; we go to a performance of *Julius Caesar*; inoculation is explained to us; we are given elaborate discussions of English literature and English science, of the speculations of Bolingbroke and the theories of Locke. The Letters may still be read with pleasure and instruction; they are written in a delightful style, running over with humour and wit, revealing here and there remarkable powers of narrative, and impregnated through and through with a wonderful mingling of gaiety, irony, and common sense. They are journalism of genius; but they are something more besides. They are informed with a high purpose, and a genuine love of humanity and the truth. The French authorities soon recognized this; they perceived that every page contained a cutting indictment of their system of government; and they adopted their usual method in such a case. The sale of the book was absolutely prohibited throughout France, and a copy of it solemnly burnt by the common hangman.

It was only gradually that the new views, of which Montesquieu and Voltaire were the principal exponents, spread their way among the public; and during the first half of the century many writers remained quite unaffected by them. Two of these—resembling each other in this fact alone, that they stood altogether outside the movement of contemporary thought—deserve our special attention.

The mantle of Racine was generally supposed to have fallen on to the shoulders of Voltaire—it had not: if it had fallen on to anyone's shoulders it was on to those of MARIVAUX. No doubt it had become diminished in the transit. Marivaux was not a great tragic writer; he was not a poet; he worked on a much smaller scale, and with far less significant material. But he was a true dramatist, a subtle psychologist, and an artist pure and simple. His comedies, too, move according to the same laws as the tragedies of Racine; they preserve the same finished symmetry of design, and leave upon the mind the same sense of unity and grace. But they are slight, etherealized, fantastic; they are Racine, as it were, by moonlight. All Marivaux's dramas pass in a world of his own invention—a world curiously compounded of imagination and reality. At first sight one can see nothing there but a kind of conventional fantasy, playing charmingly round impossible situations and queer delightful personages, who would vanish in a moment into thin air at the slightest contact with actual flesh and blood. But if Marivaux had been simply fantastic and nothing more, his achievement would have been insignificant; his great merit lies in his exquisite instinct for psychological truth. His plays are like Watteau's pictures, which, for all the unreality of their atmosphere, produce their effect owing to a mass of accurate observation and a profound sense of the realities of life. His characters, like Watteau's, seem to possess, not quite reality itself, but the very quintessence of rarefied reality—the distilled fragrance of all that is most refined, delicate and enchanting in the human spirit. His Aramintes, his Silvias, his Lucidors are purged of the grossnesses of existence; their minds and their hearts are miraculously one; in their conversations the subtleties of metaphysicians are blended with the airy clarities of birds. *Le Jeu de l'Amour et du Hasard* is perhaps the most perfect example of his work. Here the lady changes places with her waiting-maid, while the lover changes places with his valet, and, in this impossible framework of symmetrical complications, the whole action spins itself out. The beauty of the little piece depends upon the infinitely delicate art which depicts each charmingly absurd, minute transition in the process of delusion, misunderstanding, bewilderment, and explanation, with all the varieties of their interactions and shimmering personal shades. It would be difficult to find a more exquisite example of tender and discriminating fidelity to the loveliest qualities in human nature than the scene in which Silvia realizes at last that she is in love— and with whom. 'Ah! je vois clair dans mon coeur!' she exclaims at the supreme moment; and the words might stand as the epitome of the art of Marivaux. Through all the superfine convolutions of his fancies and his coquetries he never loses sight for a moment of the clear truth of the heart.

While Marivaux, to use Voltaire's phrase for him, was 'weighing nothings in scales of gossamer', a writer of a very different calibre was engaged upon one of the most forcible, one of the most actual, and one of the hugest compositions that has ever come from pen of man. The DUC DE SAINT-SIMON had spent his youth and middle life in the thick of the Court during the closing years of Louis XIV and the succeeding period of the Regency; and he occupied his old age with the compilation of his *Mémoires*. This great book offers so many points of striking contrast with the mass of French literature that it falls into a category of its own; no other work of the same outstanding merit can quite be compared to it; for it was the product of what has always been, in France, an extremely rare phenomenon—an amateur in literature who was also a genius. Saint-Simon was so far from being a professional man of letters that he would have been shocked to hear himself described as a man of letters at all; indeed, it might be said with justice that his only profession was that of a duke. It was as a duke—or, more correctly, as a *Duc et Pair*—that, in his own eyes at any rate, he lived and moved and had his being. It was round his position as a duke that the whole of his active existence had revolved; it was with the consciousness of his dukedom dominating his mind that he sat down in his retirement to write his memoirs. It might seem that no book produced in such circumstances and by such a man could possibly be valuable or interesting. But, fortunately for the world, the merit of books does not depend upon the enlightenment of authors. Saint-Simon was a man of small intellect, with medieval ideas as to the structure of society, with an absurd belief in the fundamental importance of the minutest class distinctions, and with an obsession for dukedoms almost amounting to mania: but he had in addition an incredibly passionate temperament combined with an unparalleled power of observation; and these two qualities have made his book immortal.

Besides the intrinsic merits of the work, it has the additional advantage of being concerned with an age which, of enthralling interest on its own account, also happened to be particularly suited to the capacities of the writer. If Saint-Simon had lived at any other time, his memoirs would have been admirable, no doubt, but they would have lacked the crowning excellence which they actually possess. As it was, a happy stroke of fortune placed him in the one position where he could exercise to the full his extraordinary powers: never, before or since, has there been so much to observe; never, before or since, so miraculous an observer. For, at Versailles, in the last years of Louis, Saint-Simon had before him, under his very eyes as a daily and hourly spectacle, the whole accumulated energy of France in all its manifestations; that was what he saw; and that, by the magic of his pen, is what he makes us see. Through the endless succession of his pages the enormous panorama unrolls itself, magnificent, palpitating, alive. What La Bruyère saw with the spiritual gaze of a moralist rushed upon the vision of Saint-Simon in all the colour, the detail, the intensity, the frenzy, of actual fact. He makes no comments, no reflections—or, if he does, they are ridiculous; he only sees and feels. Thus, though in the profundity of his judgement he falls so infinitely below La Bruyère, in his character-drawing he soars as high above him. His innumerable portraits are unsurpassed in literature. They spring into his pages bursting with life—individual, convincing, complete, and as various as humanity itself. He excels in that most difficult art of presenting the outward characteristics of persons, calling up before the imagination not only the details of their physical appearance, but the more recondite effects of their manner and their bearing, so that, when he has finished, one almost feels that one has met the man. But his excellence does not stop there. It is upon the inward creature that he expends his most lavish care—upon the soul that sits behind the eyelids, upon the purpose and the passion that linger in a gesture or betray themselves in a word. The joy that he takes in such descriptions soon infects the reader, who finds before long that he is being carried away by the ardour of the chase, and that at last he seizes upon the quivering quarry with all the excitement and all the fury of Saint-Simon himself. Though it would, indeed, be a mistake to suppose that Saint-Simon was always furious—the wonderful portraits of the Duchesse de Bourgogne and the Prince de Conti are in themselves sufficient to disprove that—yet there can be no doubt that his hatreds exceeded his loves, and that, in his character-drawing, he was, as it were, more at home when he detested. Then the victim is indeed dissected with a loving hand; then the details of incrimination pour out in a multitudinous stream; then the indefatigable brush of the master darkens the deepest shadows and throws the most glaring deformities into still bolder relief; then disgust, horror, pity, and ridicule finish the work which scorn and indignation had begun. Nor, in spite of the virulence of his method, do his portraits ever sink to the level of caricatures. His most malevolent exaggerations are yet so realistic that they carry conviction. When he had fashioned to his liking his terrific images—his Vendôme, his Noailles, his Pontchartrain, his Duchesse de Berry, and a hundred more—he never forgot, in the extremity of his ferocity, to commit the last insult, and to breathe into their nostrils the fatal breath of life.

And it is not simply in detached portraits that Saint-Simon's descriptive powers show themselves; they are no less remarkable in the evocation of crowded and elaborate scenes. He is a master of movement; he can make great groups of persons flow and dispose themselves and disperse again; he can produce the effect of a multitude under the dominion of some common agitation, the waves of excitement spreading in widening circles, amid the conflicting currents of curiosity and suspicion, fear and hope. He is assiduous in his descriptions of the details of places, and invariably heightens the effect of his emotional climaxes by his dramatic management of the physical *décor*. Thus his readers get to know the Versailles of that age as if they had lived in it; they are familiar with the great rooms and the long gallery; they can tell the way to the king's bedchamber, or wait by the mysterious door of Madame de Maintenon; or remember which prince had rooms opening out on to the Terrace near the Orangery, and which great family had apartments in the new wing. More than this, Saint-Simon has the art of conjuring up—often in a phrase or two—those curious intimate visions which seem to reveal the very soul of a place. How much more one knows about the extraordinary palace—how one feels the very pulse of the machine—when Saint-Simon has shown one in a flash a door opening, on a sudden, at dead of night, in an unlighted corridor, and the haughty Duc d'Harcourt stepping out among a blaze of torches, to vanish again, as swiftly as he had come, into the mysterious darkness!— Or when one has seen, amid the cold and snow of a cruel winter, the white faces of the courtiers pressed against the window-panes of the palace, as the messengers ride in from the seat of war with their dreadful catalogues of disasters and deaths!

Saint-Simon's style is the precise counterpart of his matter. It is coloured and vital to the highest degree. It is the style of a writer who does not care how many solecisms he commits—how disordered his sentences may be, how incorrect his grammar, how forced or undignified his expressions—so long as he can put on to paper in black and white the passionate vision that is in his mind. The result is something unique in French literature. If Saint-Simon had tried to write with academic correctness—and even if he had succeeded—he certainly would have spoilt his book. Fortunately, academic correctness did not interest him, while the exact delineament of his observations did. He is not afraid of using colloquialisms which every critic of the time would have shuddered at, and which, by their raciness and flavour, add enormously to his effects. His writing is also extremely metaphorical; technical terms are thrown in helter-skelter whenever the meaning would benefit; and the boldest constructions at every turn are suddenly brought into being. In describing the subtle spiritual sympathy which existed between Fénelon and Madame de Guyon he strikes out the unforgettable phrase—'leur sublime s'amalgama', which in its compression, its singularity, its vividness, reminds one rather of an English Elizabethan than a French writer of the eighteenth century. The vast movement of his sentences is particularly characteristic. Clause follows clause, image is piled upon image, the words hurry out upon one another's heels in clusters, until the construction melts away under the burning pressure of the excitement, to reform as best it may while the agitated period still expands in endless ramifications. His book is like a tropical forest—luxuriant, bewildering, enormous—with the gayest humming-birds among the branches, and the vilest monsters in the entangled grass.

Saint-Simon, so far as the influence of his contemporaries was concerned, might have been living in the Middle Ages or the moon. At a time when Voltaire's fame was ringing through Europe, he refers to him incidentally as an insignificant scribbler, and misspells his name. But the combination of such abilities and such aloofness was a singular exception, becoming, indeed, more extraordinary and improbable every day. For now the movement which had begun in the early years of the century was entering upon a new phase. The change came during the decade 1750–60, when, on the one hand, it had become obvious that all the worst features of the old regime were to be perpetuated indefinitely under the incompetent government of Louis XV, and when, on the other hand, the generation which had been brought up under the influence of Montesquieu and Voltaire came to maturity. A host of new writers, eager, positive, and resolute, burst upon the public, determined to expose to the uttermost the evils of the existing system, and, if possible, to end them. Henceforward, until the meeting of the States-General closed the period of discussion and began that of action, the movement towards reform dominated French literature, gathering in intensity as it progressed, and assuming at last the proportions and characteristics of a great organized campaign.

The ideals which animated the new writers—the *Philosophes*, as they came to be called—may be summed up in two words: Reason and Humanity. They were the heirs of that splendid spirit which had arisen in Europe at the Renaissance, which had filled Columbus when he sailed for the New World, Copernicus when he discovered the motion of the earth, and Luther when he nailed his propositions to the church door at Wittenberg. They wished to dispel the dark mass of prejudice, superstition, ignorance and folly by the clear rays of knowledge and truth; and to employ the forces of society towards the benefit of all mankind. They found in France an incompetent administration, a financial system at once futile and unjust, a barbarous judicial procedure, a blind spirit of religious intolerance—they found the traces of tyranny, caste-privilege and corruption in every branch of public life; and they found that these enormous evils were the result less of viciousness than of stupidity, less of the deliberate malice of kings or ministers than of a long, ingrained tradition of narrow-mindedness and inhumanity in the principles of government. Their great object, therefore, was to produce, by means of their writings, such an awakening of public opinion as would cause an immense transformation in the whole spirit of national life. With the actual processes of political change, with the practical details of political machinery, very few of them concerned themselves. Some of them—such as the illustrious Turgot—believed that the best way of reaching the desired improvement was through the agency of a benevolent despotism; others—such as Rousseau—had in view an elaborate, *a priori*, ideal system of government; but these were exceptions, and the majority of the *Philosophes* ignored politics proper altogether. This was a great misfortune; but it was inevitable. The beneficent changes which had been introduced so effectively and with such comparative ease into the government of England had been brought about by men of affairs; in France the men of affairs were merely the helpless tools of an autocratic machine, and the changes had to owe their origin to men uninstructed in affairs—to men of letters. Reform had to come from the outside, instead of from within; and reform of that kind spells revolution. Yet, even here, there were compensating advantages. The changes in England had been, for the most part, accomplished in a tinkering, unspeculative, hole-and-corner spirit; those in France were the result of the widest appeal to first principles, of an attempt, at any rate, to solve the fundamental problems of society, of a noble and comprehensive conception of the duties and destiny of man. This was the achievement of the *Philosophes*. They spread far and wide, not only through France, but through the whole civilized world, a multitude of searching interrogations on the most vital subjects; they propounded vast theories, they awoke new enthusiasms, and uplifted new ideals. In two directions particularly their influence has been enormous. By their insistence on the right of free opinion and on the paramount necessity of free speculation, untrammelled by the fetters of orthodoxy and tradition, they established once for all as the common property of the human race that scientific spirit which has had such an immense effect on modern civilization, and whose full import we are still only just beginning to understand. And, owing mainly to their efforts also, the spirit of humanity has come to be an abiding influence in the world. It was they who, by their relentless exposure of the abuses of the French judicial system—the scandal of arbitrary imprisonment, the futile barbarism of torture, the medieval abominations of the penal code—finally instilled into public opinion a hatred of cruelty and injustice in all their forms; it was they who denounced the horrors of the slave-trade; it was they who unceasingly lamented the awful evils of war. So far as the actual content of their thought was concerned, they were not great originators. The germs of their most fruitful theories they found elsewhere—chiefly among the thinkers of England; and, when they attempted original thinking on their own account, though they were bold and ingenious, they were apt also to be crude. In some sciences—political economy, for instance, and psychology—they led the way, but attained to no lasting achievement. They suffered from the same faults as Montesquieu in his *Esprit des Lois*. In their love of pure reason, they relied too often on the swift processes of argument for the solution of difficult problems, and omitted that patient investigation of premises upon which the validity of all argument depends. They were too fond of systems, and those neatly constructed logical theories into which everything may be fitted admirably—except the facts. In addition, the lack of psychological insight which was so common in the eighteenth century tended to narrow their sympathies; and in particular they failed to realize the beauty and significance of religious and mystical states of mind. These defects eventually produced a reaction against their teaching—a reaction during which the true value of their work was for a time obscured. For that value is not to be looked for in the enunciation of certain definite doctrines, but in something much wider and more profound. The *Philosophes* were important not so much for the answers which they gave as for the questions which they asked; their real originality lay not in their thought, but in their spirit. They were the first great popularizers. Other men before them had thought more accurately and more deeply; they were the first to fling the light of thought wide through the world, to appeal, not to the scholar and the specialist, but to the ordinary man and woman, and to proclaim the glories of civilization as the heritage of all humanity. Above all, they instilled a new spirit into the speculations of men—the spirit of hope. They believed ardently in the fundamental goodness of mankind, and they looked forward into the future with the certain expectation of the ultimate triumph of what was best. Though in some directions their sympathies were limited, their love of humanity was a profound and genuine feeling which moved them to a boundless enthusiasm. Though their faith in creeds was small, their faith in mankind was great. The spirit which filled them was well shown when, during the darkest days of the Terror, the noble Condorcet, in the hiding-place from which he came forth only to die, wrote his historical *Sketch of the Progress of the Human Mind*, with its final chapter foretelling the future triumphs of reason, and asserting the unlimited perfectibility of man.

The energies of the *Philosophes* were given a centre and a rallying-point by the great undertaking of the *Encyclopaedia*, the publication of which covered a period of thirty years (1751–80). The object of this colossal work, which contained a survey of human activity in all its branches—political, scientific, artistic, philosophical, commercial—was to record in a permanent and concentrated form the advance of civilization. A multitude of writers contributed to it, of varying merit and of various opinions, but all animated by the new belief in reason and humanity. The ponderous volumes are not great literature; their importance lies in the place which they fill in the progress of thought, and in their immense influence in the propagation of the new spirit. In spite of its bulk the book was extremely successful; edition after edition was printed; the desire to know and to think began to permeate through all the grades of society. Nor was it only in France that these effects were visible; the prestige of French literature and French manners carried the teaching of the *Philosophes* all over Europe; great princes and ministers—Frederick in Prussia, Catherine in Russia, Pombal in Portugal—eagerly joined the swelling current; enlightenment was abroad in the world.

The *Encyclopaedia* would never have come into existence without the genius, the energy, and the enthusiasm of one man—DIDEROT. In him the spirit of the age found its most typical expression. He was indeed *the Philosophe*—more completely than all the rest universal, brilliant, inquisitive, sceptical, generous, hopeful, and humane. It was he who originated the *Encyclopaedia*, who, in company with Dalembert, undertook its editorship, and who, eventually alone, accomplished the herculean task of bringing the great production, in spite of obstacle after obstacle—in spite of government prohibitions, lack of funds, desertions, treacheries, and the mischances of thirty years—to a triumphant conclusion. This was the work of his life; and it was work which, by its very nature, could leave—except for that long row of neglected volumes—no lasting memorial. But the superabundant spirit of Diderot was not content with that: in the intervals of this stupendous labour, which would have exhausted to their last fibre the energies of a lesser man, he found time not only to pour out a constant flow of writing in a multitude of miscellaneous forms—in dramas, in art criticism, in philosophical essays, and in a voluminous correspondence—but also to create on the sly as it were, and without a thought of publication, two or three finished masterpieces which can never be forgotten. Of these, the most important is *Le Neveu de Rameau*, where Diderot's whole soul gushes out in one clear, strong, sparkling jet of incomparable prose. In the sheer enchantment of its vitality this wonderful little book has certainly never been surpassed. It enthrals the reader as completely as the most exciting romance, or the talk of some irresistibly brilliant *raconteur*. Indeed, the writing, with its ease, its vigour, its colour, and its rapidity, might almost be taken for what, in fact, it purports to be—conversation put into print, were it not for the magical perfection of its form. Never did a style combine more absolutely the movement of life with the serenity of art. Every sentence is exciting, and every sentence is beautiful. The book must have been composed quickly, without effort, almost off-hand; but the mind that composed it was the mind of a master, who, even as he revelled in the joyous manifestation of his genius, preserved, with an instinctive power, the master's control. In truth, beneath the gay galaxies of scintillating thoughts that strew the pages, one can discern the firm, warm, broad substance of Diderot's very self, underlying and supporting all. That is the real subject of a book which seems to have taken all subjects for its province—from the origin of music to the purpose of the universe; and the central figure—the queer, delightful, Bohemian Rameau, evoked for us with such a marvellous distinctness—is in fact no more than the reed with many stops through which Diderot is blowing. Of all his countrymen, he comes nearest, in spirit and in manner, to the great Curé of Meudon. The rich, exuberant, intoxicating tones of Rabelais vibrate in his voice. He has—not all, for no son of man will ever again have that; but he has *some* of Rabelais' stupendous breadth, and he has yet more of Rabelais' enormous optimism. His complete materialism—his disbelief in any Providence or any immortality—instead of depressing him, seems rather to have given fresh buoyancy to his spirit; if this life on earth were all, that only served, in his eyes, to redouble the intensity of its value. And his enthusiasm inspired him with a philanthropy unknown to Rabelais—an active benevolence that never tired. For indeed he was, above all else, a man of his own age: a man who could think subtly and work nobly as well as write splendidly; who could weep as well as laugh. He is, perhaps, a smaller figure than Rabelais; but he is much nearer to ourselves. And, when we have come to the end of his generous pages, the final impression that is left with us is of a man whom we cannot choose but love.

Besides Diderot, the band of the *Philosophes* included many famous names. There was the brilliant and witty mathematician, Dalembert; there was the grave and noble statesman, Turgot; there was the psychologist, Condillac; there was the light, good-humoured Marmontel; there was the penetrating and ill-fated Condorcet. Helvétius and D'Holbach plunged boldly into ethics and metaphysics; while, a little apart, in learned repose, Buffon advanced the purest interests of science by his researches in Natural History. As every year passed there were new accessions to this great array of writers, who waged their war against ignorance and prejudice with an ever-increasing fury. A war indeed it was. On one side were all the forces of intellect; on the other was all the mass of entrenched and powerful dullness. In reply to the brisk fire of the *Philosophes*—argument, derision, learning, wit—the authorities in State and Church opposed the more serious artillery of censorships, suppressions, imprisonments, and exiles. There was hardly an eminent writer in Paris who was unacquainted with the inside of the Conciergerie or the Bastille. It was only natural, therefore, that the struggle should have become a highly embittered one, and that at times, in the heat of it, the party whose watchword was a hatred of fanaticism should have grown itself fanatical. But it was clear that the powers of reaction were steadily losing ground; they could only assert themselves spasmodically; their hold upon public opinion was slipping away. Thus the efforts of the band of writers in Paris seemed about to be crowned with success. But this result had not been achieved by their efforts alone. In the midst of the conflict they had received the aid of a powerful auxiliary, who had thrown himself with the utmost vigour into the struggle, and, far as he was from the centre of operations, had assumed supreme command.

It was Voltaire. This great man had now entered upon the final, and by far the most important, period of his astonishing career. It is a curious fact that if Voltaire had died at the age of sixty he would now only be remembered as a writer of talent and versatility, who had given conspicuous evidence, in one or two works, of a liberal and brilliant intelligence, but who had enjoyed a reputation in his own age, as a poet and dramatist, infinitely beyond his deserts. He entered upon the really significant period of his activity at an age when most men have already sought repose. Nor was this all; for, by a singular stroke of fortune, his existence was prolonged far beyond the common span; so that, in spite of the late hour of its beginning, the most fruitful and important epoch of his life extended over a quarter of a century (1754–78). That he ever entered upon this last period of his career seems in itself to have depended as much on accident as his fateful residence in England. After the publication of the *Lettres Philosophiques*, he had done very little to fulfil the promise of that work. He had retired to the country house of Madame du Châtelet, where he had devoted himself to science, play-writing, and the preparation of a universal history. His reputation had increased; for it was in these years that he produced his most popular tragedies—*Zaïre, Mérope, Alzire*, and *Mahomet*—while a correspondence carried on in the most affectionate terms with Frederick the Great yet further added to his prestige; but his essential genius still remained quiescent. Then at last Madame du Châtelet died and Voltaire took the great step of his life. At the invitation of Frederick he left France, and went to live as a pensioner of the Prussian king in the palace at Potsdam. But his stay there did not last long. It seemed as if the two most remarkable men in Europe liked each other so well that they could not remain apart—and so ill that they could not remain together. After a year or two, there was the inevitable explosion. Voltaire fled from Prussia, giving to the world before he did so one of the most amusing *jeux d'esprit* ever written—the celebrated *Diatribe du Docteur Akakia*—and, after some hesitation, settled down near the Lake of Geneva. A few years later he moved into the *château* of Ferney, which became henceforward his permanent abode.

Voltaire was now sixty years of age. His position was an enviable one. His reputation was very great, and he had amassed a considerable fortune, which not only assured him complete independence, but enabled him to live in his domains on the large and lavish scale of a country magnate. His residence at Ferney, just on the border of French territory, put him beyond the reach of government interference, while he was yet not too far distant to be out of touch with the capital. Thus the opportunity had at last come for the full display of his powers. And those powers were indeed extraordinary. His character was composed of a strange amalgam of all the most contradictory elements in human nature, and it would be difficult to name a single virtue or a single vice which he did not possess. He was the most egotistical of mortals, and the most disinterested; he was graspingly avaricious, and profusely generous; he was treacherous, mischievous, frivolous, and mean, yet he was a firm friend and a true benefactor, yet he was profoundly serious and inspired by the noblest enthusiasms. Nature had carried these contradictions even into his physical constitution. His health was so bad that he seemed to pass his whole life on the brink of the grave; nevertheless his vitality has probably never been surpassed in the history of the world. Here, indeed, was the one characteristic which never deserted him: he was always active with an insatiable activity; it was always safe to say of him that, whatever else he was, he was not at rest. His long, gaunt body, frantically gesticulating, his skull-like face, with its mobile features twisted into an eternal grin, its piercing eyes sparkling and darting—all this suggested the appearance of a corpse galvanized into an incredible animation. But in truth it was no dead ghost that inhabited this strange tenement, but the fierce and powerful spirit of an intensely living man.

Some signs had already appeared of the form which his activity was now about to take. During his residence in Prussia he had completed his historical *Essai sur les Moeurs*, which passed over in rapid review the whole development of humanity, and closed with a brilliant sketch of the age of Louis XIV. This work was highly original in many ways. It was the first history which attempted to describe the march of civilization in its broadest aspects, which included a consideration of the great Eastern peoples, which dealt rather with the progress of the arts and the sciences than with the details of politics and wars. But its chief importance lay in the fact that it was in reality, under its historical trappings, a work of propaganda. It was a counterblast to Bossuet's *Histoire Universelle*. That book had shown the world's history as a part of the providential order—a grand unfolding of design. Voltaire's view was very different. To him, as to Montesquieu, natural causes alone were operative in history; but this was not all; in his eyes there was one influence which, from the earliest ages, had continually retarded the progress of humanity, and that influence was religious belief. Thus his book, though far more brilliant and far more modern than that of Bossuet, was nevertheless almost equally biased. It was history with a thesis, and the gibe of Montesquieu was justifiable. 'Voltaire,' he said, 'writes history to glorify his own convent, like any Benedictine monk.' Voltaire's 'convent' was the philosophical school in Paris; and his desire to glorify it was soon to appear in other directions.

The *Essai sur les Moeurs* is an exceedingly amusing narrative, but it is a long and learned work filling several volumes, and the fruit of many years of research. Voltaire was determined henceforward to distil its spirit into more compendious and popular forms. He had no more time for elaborate dissertations; he must reach the public by quicker and surer ways. Accordingly there now began to pour into Paris a flood of short light booklets—essays, plays, poems, romances, letters, tracts—a multitude of writings infinitely varied in form and scope, but all equally irresistible and all equally bearing the unmistakable signs of their origin at Ferney. Voltaire's inimitable style had at last found a medium in which it could display itself in all its charm and all its brilliance. The pointed, cutting, mocking sentences laugh and dance through his pages like light-toed, prick-eared elves. Once seen, and there is no help for it—one must follow, into whatever dangerous and unknown regions those magic imps may lead. The pamphlets were of course forbidden, but without effect; they were sold in thousands, and new cargoes, somehow or other, were always slipping across the frontier from Holland or Geneva. Whenever a particularly outrageous one appeared, Voltaire wrote off to all his friends to assure them that he knew nothing whatever of the production, that it was probably a translation from the work of an English clergyman, and that, in short, everyone would immediately see from the style alone that it was—*not* his. An endless series of absurd pseudonyms intensified the farce. Oh no! Voltaire was certainly not the author of this scandalous book. How could he be? Did not the title-page plainly show that it was the work of Frère Cucufin, or the uncle of Abbé Bazin, or the Comte de Boulainvilliers, or the Emperor of China? And so the game proceeded; and so all France laughed; and so all France read.

Two forms of this light literature Voltaire made especially his own. He brought the Dialogue to perfection; for the form suited him exactly, with its opportunities for the rapid exposition of contrary doctrines, for the humorous stultification of opponents, and for witty repartee. Into this mould he has poured some of his finest materials; and in such pieces as *Le Dîner du Comte de Boulainvilliers* and *Frère Rigolet et l'Empereur de la Chine* one finds the concentrated essence of his whole work. Equally effective and equally characteristic is the *Dictionnaire Philosophique*, which contains a great number of very short miscellaneous articles arranged in alphabetical order. This plan gave Voltaire complete freedom both in the choice of subjects and in their manipulation; as the spirit seized him he could fly out into a page of sarcasm or speculation or criticism or buffoonery, and such liberty was precisely to his taste; so that the book which had first appeared as a pocket dictionary—'ce diable de portatif', he calls it in a letter proving quite conclusively that *he*, at any rate, was not responsible for the wretched thing—were there not Hebrew quotations in it? and who could accuse him of knowing Hebrew?—had swollen to six volumes before he died.

The subjects of these writings were very various. Ostensibly, at least, they were by no means limited to matters of controversy. Some were successful tragedies, others were pieces of criticism, others were historical essays, others were frivolous short stories, or *vers de société*.

But, in all of them, somewhere or other, the cloven hoof was bound to show itself at last. Whatever disguises he might assume, Voltaire in reality was always writing for his 'convent'; he was pressing forward, at every possible opportunity, the great movement against the old régime. His attack covers a wide ground. The abuses of the financial system, the defects in the administration of justice, the futility of the restraints upon trade—upon these and a hundred similar subjects he poured out an incessant torrent of gay, penetrating, frivolous and remorseless words. But there was one theme to which he was perpetually recurring, which forms the subject for his bitterest jests, and which, in fact, dominates the whole of his work, 'Écrasez l'infame!' was his constant exclamation; and the 'infamous thing' which he wished to see stamped underfoot was nothing less than religion. The extraordinary fury of his attack on religion has, in the eyes of many, imprinted an indelible stigma upon his name; but the true nature of his position in this matter has often been misunderstood, and deserves some examination.

Voltaire was a profoundly irreligious man. In this he resembled the majority of his contemporaries; but he carried the quality perhaps to a further pitch than any man of his age. For, with him, it was not merely the purely religious and mystical feelings that were absent; he lacked all sympathy with those vague, brooding, emotional states of mind which go to create the highest forms of poetry, music, and art, and which are called forth into such a moving intensity by the beauties of Nature. These things Voltaire did not understand; he did not even perceive them; for him, in fact, they did not exist; and the notion that men could be influenced by them, genuinely and deeply, he considered to be so absurd as hardly to need discussion. This was certainly a great weakness in him—a great limitation of spirit. It has vitiated a large part of his writings; and it has done more than that—it has obscured, to many of his readers, the real nature and the real value of his work. For, combined with this inability to comprehend some of the noblest parts of man's nature, Voltaire possessed other qualities of high importance which went far to compensate for his defects. If he was blind to some truths, he perceived others with wonderful clearness; if his sympathies in some directions were atrophied, in others they were sensitive to an extraordinary degree. In the light of these considerations his attitude towards religion becomes easier to understand. All the highest elements of religion—the ardent devotion, the individual ecstasy, the sense of communion with the divine—these things he simply ignored. But, unfortunately, in his day there was a side of religion which, with his piercing clear-sightedness, he could not ignore. The spirit of fanaticism was still lingering in France; it was the spirit which had burst out on the Eve of St. Bartholomew, and had dictated the fatal Revocation of the Edict of Nantes. In every branch of life its influence was active, infusing prejudice, bitterness, and strife; but its effects were especially terrible in the administration of justice. It so happened that while Voltaire was at Ferney some glaring instances of this dreadful fact came to light. A young Protestant named Calas committed suicide in Toulouse, and, owing to the blind zealotry of the magistrates of the town, his father, completely innocent, was found guilty of his murder and broken on the wheel. Shortly afterwards, another Protestant, Sirven, was condemned in similar circumstances, but escaped to Ferney. A few years later, two youths of seventeen were convicted at Abbeville for making some profane jokes. Both were condemned to have their tongues torn out and to be decapitated; one managed to escape, the other was executed. That such things could happen in eighteenth-century France seems incredible; but happen they did, and who knows how many more of a like atrocity? The fact that these three came to light at all was owing to Voltaire himself. But for his penetration, his courage, and his skill, the terrible murder of Calas would to this day have remained unknown, and the dreadful affair of Abbeville would have been forgotten in a month. Different men respond most readily to different stimuli: the spectacle of cruelty and injustice bit like a lash into the nerves of Voltaire, and plunged him into an agony of horror. He resolved never to rest until he had not only obtained reparation for these particular acts of injustice, but had rooted out for ever from men's minds the superstitious bigotry which made them possible. It was to attain this end that he attacked with such persistence and such violence all religion and all priestcraft in general, and, in particular, the orthodox dogmas of the Roman Catholic Church. It became the great object of his life to convince public opinion that those dogmas were both ridiculous and contemptible in themselves, and abominable in their results. In this we may think him right or we may think him wrong; our judgement will depend upon the nature of our own opinions. But, whatever our opinions, we cannot think him wicked; for we cannot doubt that the one dominating motive in all that he wrote upon the subject of religion was a passionate desire for the welfare of mankind.

Voltaire's philosophical views were curious. While he entirely discarded the miraculous from his system, he nevertheless believed in a Deity—a supreme First Cause of all the phenomena of the universe. Yet, when he looked round upon the world as it was, the evil and the misery in it were what seized his attention and appalled his mind. The optimism of so many of his contemporaries appeared to him a shallow crude doctrine unrelated to the facts of existence, and it was to give expression to this view that he composed the most famous of all his works—*Candide*. This book, outwardly a romance of the most flippant kind, contains in reality the essence of Voltaire's maturest reflections upon human life. It is a singular fact that a book which must often have been read simply for the sake of its wit and its impropriety should nevertheless be one of the bitterest and most melancholy that was ever written. But it is a safe rule to make, that Voltaire's meaning is deep in proportion to the lightness of his writing—that it is when he is most in earnest that he grins most. And, in *Candide*, the brilliance and the seriousness alike reach their climax. The book is a catalogue of all the woes, all the misfortunes, all the degradations, and all the horrors that can afflict humanity; and throughout it Voltaire's grin is never for a moment relaxed. As catastrophe follows catastrophe, and disaster succeeds disaster, not only does he laugh himself consumedly, but he makes his reader laugh no less; and it is only when the book is finished that the true meaning of it is borne in upon the mind. Then it is that the scintillating pages begin to exercise their grim unforgettable effect; and the pettiness and misery of man seem to borrow a new intensity from the relentless laughter of Voltaire.

But perhaps the most wonderful thing about *Candide* is that it contains, after all, something more than mere pessimism—it contains a positive doctrine as well. Voltaire's common sense withers the Ideal; but it remains common sense. 'Il faut cultiver notre jardin' is his final word—one of the very few pieces of practical wisdom ever uttered by a philosopher.

Voltaire's style reaches the summit of its perfection in *Candide*; but it is perfect in all that he wrote. His prose is the final embodiment of the most characteristic qualities of the French genius. If all that that great nation had ever done or thought were abolished from the world, except a single sentence of Voltaire's, the essence of their achievement would have survived. His writing brings to a culmination the tradition that Pascal had inaugurated in his *Lettres Provinciales*: clarity, simplicity and wit—these supreme qualities it possesses in an unequalled degree. But these qualities, pushed to an extreme, have also their disadvantages. Voltaire's style is narrow; it is like a rapier—all point; with such neatness, such lightness, the sweeping blade of Pascal has become an impossibility. Compared to the measured march of Bossuet's sentences, Voltaire's sprightly periods remind one almost of a pirouette. But the pirouette is Voltaire's—executed with all the grace, all the ease, all the latent strength of a consummate dancer; it would be folly to complain; yet it was clear that a reaction was bound to follow—and a salutary reaction. Signs of it were already visible in the colour and passion of Diderot's writing; but it was not until the nineteenth century that the great change came.

Nowhere is the excellence of Voltaire's style more conspicuous than in his Correspondence, which forms so large and important a portion of his work. A more delightful and a more indefatigable letter-writer never lived. The number of his published letters exceeds ten thousand; how many more he may actually have written one hardly ventures to imagine, for the great majority of those that have survived date only from the last thirty years of his long life. The collection is invaluable alike for the light which it throws upon Voltaire's career and character, and for the extent to which it reflects the manners, sentiments, and thought of the age. For Voltaire corresponded with all Europe. His reputation, already vast before he settled at Ferney, rose after that date to a well-nigh incredible height. No man had wielded such an influence since the days when Bernard of Clairvaux dictated the conduct of popes and princes from his monastic cell. But, since then, the wheel had indeed come full circle! The very antithesis of the Middle Ages was personified in the strange old creature who in his lordly retreat by the Lake of Geneva alternately coquetted with empresses, received the homage of statesmen and philosophers, domineered over literature in all its branches, and laughed Mother Church to scorn. As the years advanced, Voltaire's industry, which had always been astonishing, continually increased. As if his intellectual interests were not enough to occupy him, he took to commercial enterprise, developed the resources of his estates, and started a successful colony of watchmakers at Ferney. Every day he worked for long hours at his desk, spinning his ceaseless web of tracts, letters, tragedies, and farces. In the evening he would discharge the functions of a munificent host, entertain the whole neighbourhood with balls and suppers, and take part in one of his own tragedies on the stage of his private theatre. Then a veritable frenzy would seize upon him; shutting himself up in his room for days together, he would devote every particle of his terrific energies to the concoction of some devastating dialogue, or some insidious piece of profanation for his *Dictionnaire Philosophique*. At length his fragile form would sink exhausted—he would be dying—he would be dead; and next morning he would be up again as brisk as ever, directing the cutting of the crops.

One day, quite suddenly, he appeared in Paris, which he had not visited for nearly thirty years. His arrival was the signal for one of the most extraordinary manifestations of enthusiasm that the world has ever seen. For some weeks he reigned in the capital, visible and glorious, the undisputed lord of the civilized universe. The climax came when he appeared in a box at the Théâtre Français, to witness a performance of the latest of his tragedies, and the whole house rose as one man to greet him. His triumph seemed to be something more than the mere personal triumph of a frail old mortal; it seemed to be the triumph of all that was noblest in the aspirations of the human race. But the fatigue and excitement of those weeks proved too much even for Voltaire in the full flush of his eighty-fourth year. An overdose of opium completed what Nature had begun; and the amazing being rested at last.

French literature during the latter half of the eighteenth century was rich in striking personalities. It might have been expected that an age which had produced both Diderot and Voltaire would hardly be able to boast of yet another star of equal magnitude. But, in JEAN-JACQUES ROUSSEAU, there appeared a man in some ways even more remarkable than either of his great contemporaries. The peculiar distinction of Rousseau was his originality. Neither Voltaire nor Diderot possessed this quality in a supreme degree. Voltaire, indeed, can only claim to be original by virtue of his overwhelming common sense, which enabled him to see clearly what others could only see confusedly, to strike without fear where others were only willing to wound; but the whole bulk of his thought really rested on the same foundation as that which supported the ordinary conceptions of the average man of the day. Diderot was a far bolder, a far more speculative thinker; but yet, though he led the very van of the age, he was always in it; his originality was never more than a development—though it was often an extreme development—of the ideas that lay around him. Rousseau's originality went infinitely further than this. He neither represented his age, nor led it; he opposed it. His outlook upon the world was truly revolutionary. In his eyes, the reforms which his contemporaries were so busy introducing into society were worse than useless—the mere patching of an edifice which would never be fit to live in. He believed that it was necessary to start altogether afresh. And what makes him so singularly interesting a figure is that, in more than one sense, he was right. It *was* necessary to start afresh; and the new world which was to spring from the old one was to embody, in a multitude of ways, the visions of Rousseau. He was a prophet, with the strange inspiration of a prophet—and the dishonour in his own country.

But inspiration and dishonour are not the only characteristics of prophets: as a rule, they are also highly confused in the delivery of their prophecies; and Rousseau was no exception. In his writings, the true gist of his meaning seems to be only partially revealed; and it is clear that he himself was never really aware of the fundamental notions that lay at the back of his thought. Hence nothing can be easier than to pull his work to pieces, and to demonstrate beyond a doubt that it is full of fallacies, inconsistencies, and absurdities. It is very easy to point out that the *Control Social* is a miserable piece of logic-chopping, to pour scorn on the stilted sentiment and distorted morality of *La Nouvelle Héloïse*, and finally to draw a cutting comparison between Rousseau's preaching and his practice, as it stands revealed in the *Confessions*—the lover of independence who never earned his own living, the apostle of equality who was a snob, and the educationist who left his children in the Foundling Hospital. All this has often been done, and no doubt will often be done again; but it is futile. Rousseau lives, and will live, a vast and penetrating influence, in spite of all his critics. There is something in him that eludes their foot-rules. It is so difficult to take the measure of a soul!

Difficult, indeed; for, if we examine the doctrine that seems to be Rousseau's fundamental one—that, at least, on which he himself lays most stress—here, too, we shall find a mass of error. Rousseau was perpetually advocating the return to Nature. All the great evils from which humanity suffers are, he declared, the outcome of civilization; the ideal man is the primitive man—the untutored Indian, innocent, chaste, brave, who adores the Creator of the universe in simplicity, and passes his life in virtuous harmony with the purposes of Nature. If we cannot hope to reach quite that height of excellence, let us at least try to get as near it as we can. So far from pressing on the work of civilization, with the *Philosophes*, let us try to forget that we are civilized and be natural instead. This was the burden of Rousseau's teaching, and it was founded on a complete misconception of the facts. The noble Indian was a myth. The more we find out about primitive man, the more certain it becomes that, so far from being the ideal creature of Rousseau's imagination, he was in reality a savage whose whole life was dominated, on the one hand by the mere brute necessities of existence, and on the other by a complicated and revolting system of superstitions. Nature is neither simple nor good; and all history shows that the necessary condition for the production of any of the really valuable things of life is the control of Nature by man—in fact, civilization. So far, therefore, the *Philosophes* were right; if the Golden Age was to have any place at all in the story of humanity, it must be, not at the beginning, but the end.

But Rousseau was not, at bottom, concerned with the truth of any historical theory at all. It was only because he hated the present that he idealized the past. His primitive Golden Age was an imaginary refuge from the actual world of the eighteenth century. What he detested and condemned in that world was in reality not civilization, but the conventionality of civilization—the restrictions upon the free play of the human spirit which seemed to be inherent in civilized life. The strange feeling of revolt that surged up within him when he contemplated the drawing-rooms of Paris, with their brilliance and their philosophy, their intellect and their culture, arose from a profounder cause than a false historical theory, or a defective logical system, or a mean personal jealousy and morbid pride. All these elements, no doubt, entered into his feeling—for Rousseau was a very far from perfect human being; but the ultimate source was beyond and below them—in his instinctive, overmastering perception of the importance and the dignity of the individual soul. It was in this perception that Rousseau's great originality lay. His revolt was a spiritual revolt. In the Middle Ages the immense significance of the human spirit had been realized, but it had been inextricably involved in a mass of theological superstition. The eighteenth century, on the other hand, had achieved the great conception of a secular system of society; but, in doing so, it had left out of account the spiritual nature of man, who was regarded simply as a rational animal in an organized social group. Rousseau was the first to unite the two views, to revive the medieval theory of the soul without its theological trappings, and to believe—half unconsciously, perhaps, and yet with a profound conviction—that the individual, now, on this earth, and in himself, was the most important thing in the world.

This belief, no doubt, would have arisen in Europe, in some way or other, if Rousseau had never lived; but it was he who clothed it with the splendour of genius, and, by the passion of his utterance, sowed it far and wide in the hearts of men. In two directions his influence was enormous. His glowing conception of individual dignity and individual rights as adhering, not to a privileged few, but to the whole mass of humanity, seized upon the imagination of France, supplied a new and potent stimulus to the movement towards political change, and produced a deep effect upon the development of the Revolution. But it is in literature, and those emotions of real life which find their natural outlet in literature, that the influence of Rousseau's spirit may be most clearly seen.

It is often lightly stated that the eighteenth century was an unemotional age. What, it is asked, could be more frigid than the poetry of Pope? Or more devoid of true feeling than the mockery of Voltaire? But such a view is a very superficial one; and it is generally held by persons who have never given more than a hasty glance at the works they are so ready to condemn. It is certainly true that at first sight Pope's couplets appear to be cold and mechanical; but if we look more closely we shall soon find that these apparently monotonous verses have been made the vehicle for some of the most passionate feelings of disgust and animosity that ever agitated a human breast. As for Voltaire, we have already seen that to infer lack of feeling from his epigrams and laughter would be as foolish as to infer that a white-hot bar of molten steel lacked heat because it was not red. The accusation is untenable; the age that produced—to consider French literature alone—a Voltaire, a Diderot, and a Saint-Simon cannot be called an age without emotion. Yet it is clear that, in the matter of emotion, a distinction of some sort does exist between that age and this. The distinction lies not so much in the emotion itself as in the *attitude towards* emotion, adopted by the men of those days and by ourselves. In the eighteenth century men were passionate—intensely passionate; but they were passionate almost unconsciously, in a direct unreflective way. If anyone had asked Voltaire to analyse his feelings accurately, he would have replied that he had other things to think about; the notion of paying careful attention to mere feelings would have seemed to him ridiculous. And, when Saint-Simon sat down to write his Memoirs, it never occurred to him for a moment to give any real account of what, in all the highly personal transactions that he describes, he intimately felt. He tells us nothing of his private life; he mentions his wife once, and almost apologizes for doing so; really, could a gentleman—a duke—dwell upon such matters, and preserve his self-respect? But, to us, it is precisely such matters that form the pivot of a personality—the index of a soul. A man's feelings are his very self, and it is around them that all that is noblest and profoundest in our literature seems naturally to centre. A great novelist is one who can penetrate and describe the feelings of others; a great poet is one who can invest his own with beauty and proclaim them to the world. We have come to set a value upon introspection which was quite unknown in the eighteenth century—unknown, that is, until Rousseau, in the most valuable and characteristic of his works—his *Confessions*— started the vast current in literature and in sentiment which is still flowing to-day. The *Confessions* is the detailed, intimate, complete history of a soul. It describes Rousseau's life, from its beginning until its maturity, from the most personal point of view, with no disguises or reticences of any kind. It is written with great art. Rousseau's style, like his matter, foreshadows the future; his periods are cast in a looser, larger, more oratorical mould than those of his contemporaries; his sentences are less fiery and excitable; though he can be witty when he wishes, he is never frivolous; and a tone of earnest intimate passion lingers in his faultless rhythms. With his great powers of expression he combined a wonderful aptitude for the perception of the subtlest shades of feeling and of mood. He was sensitive to an extraordinary degree—with the sensitiveness of a proud, shy nature, unhardened by the commerce of the world. There is, indeed, an unpleasant side to his *Confessions*. Rousseau, like most explorers, became obsessed by his own discoveries; he pushed the introspective method to its farthest limits; the sanctity of the individual seemed to him not only to dignify the slightest idiosyncrasies of temperament and character, but also, in some sort of way, to justify what was positively bad. Thus his book contains the germs of that Byronic egotism which later became the fashion all over Europe. It is also, in parts, a morbid book. Rousseau was not content to extenuate nothing; his failings got upon his nerves; and, while he was ready to dilate upon them himself with an infinite wealth of detail, the slightest hint of a reflection on his conduct from any other person filled him with an agony and a rage which, at the end of his life, developed into madness. To strict moralists, therefore, and to purists in good taste, the *Confessions* will always be unpalatable. More indulgent readers will find in those pages the traces of a spirit which, with all its faults, its errors, its diseases, deserves something more than pity—deserves almost love. At any rate, it is a spirit singularly akin to our own. Out of the far-off, sharp, eager, unpoetical, unpsychological eighteenth century, it speaks to us in the familiar accents of inward contemplation, of brooding reminiscence, of subtly-shifting temperament, of quiet melancholy, of visionary joy. Rousseau, one feels, was the only man of his age who ever wanted to be alone. He understood that luxury: understood the fascination of silence, and the loveliness of dreams. He understood, too, the exquisite suggestions of Nature, and he never wrote more beautifully than when he was describing the gentle process of her influences on the solitary human soul. He understood simplicity: the charm of little happinesses, the sweetness of ordinary affections, the beauty of a country face. The paradox is strange; how was it that it should have been left to the morbid, tortured, half-crazy egoist of the *Confessions* to lead the way to such spiritual delicacies, such innocent delights?

The paradox was too strange for Rousseau's contemporaries. They could not understand him. His works were highly popular; he was received into the most brilliant circles in Paris; he made friends with the most eminent men of the day; and then ensued misunderstandings, accusations, quarrels, and at last complete disaster. Rousseau vanished from society, driven out, according to his account, by the treacheries of his friends; the victim, according to their account, of his own petty jealousies and morbid suspicions. At every point in the quarrel, his friends, and such great and honest men as Diderot and Hume were among them, seem to have been in the right; but it seems no less clear that they were too anxious to proclaim and emphasize the faults of a poor, unfortunate, demented man. We can hardly blame them; for, in their eyes, Rousseau appeared as a kind of mad dog—a pest to society, deserving of no quarter. They did not realize—they *could* not—that beneath the meanness and the frenzy that were so obvious to them was the soul of a poet and a seer. The wretched man wandered for long in Switzerland, in Germany, in England, pursued by the ever-deepening shadows of his maniacal suspicions. At last he returned to France, to end his life, after years of lingering misery, in obscurity and despair.

Rousseau and Voltaire both died in 1778—hardly more than ten years before the commencement of the Revolution. Into that last decade of the old régime there seemed to be concentrated all the ardour, all the hope, all the excitement, all the brilliance of the preceding century. Had not Reason and Humanity triumphed at last? Triumphed, at any rate, in spirit; for who was not converted? All that remained now was the final, quick, easy turn which would put into action the words of the philosophers and make this earth a paradise. And still new visions kept opening out before the eyes of enthusiasts—strange speculations and wondrous possibilities. The march of mind seemed so rapid that the most advanced thinkers of yesterday were already out of date. 'Voltaire est bigot: il est déiste,' exclaimed one of the wits of Paris, and the sentiment expressed the general feeling of untrammelled mental freedom and swift progression which was seething all over the country. It was at this moment that the production of BEAUMARCHAIS' brilliant comedy, *Le Mariage de Figaro*, electrified the intellectual public of Versailles and the capital. In that play the old régime was presented, not in the dark colours of satire, but under the sparkling light of frivolity, gaiety, and idleness—a vision of endless intrigue and vapid love-making among the antiquated remains of feudal privileges and social caste. In this fairyland one being alone has reality—Figaro, the restless, fiendishly clever, nondescript valet, sprung from no one knows where, destined to no one knows what, but gradually emerging a strange and sinister profile among the laughter and the flowers. 'What have you done, Monsieur le Comte,' he bursts out at last to his master, 'to deserve all these advantages?—I know. *Vous vous êtes donné la peine de naître!*' In that sentence one can hear—far off, but distinct—the flash and snap of the guillotine. To those happy listeners, though, no such sound was audible. Their speculations went another way. All was roseate, all was charming as the coaches dashed through the narrow streets of Paris, carrying their finely-powdered ladies and gentlemen, in silks and jewels, to the assemblies of the night. Within, the candles sparkled, and the diamonds, and the eyes of the company, sitting round in gilded delicate chairs. And then there was supper, and the Marquise was witty, and the Comte was sententious, while yet newer vistas opened of yet happier worlds, dancing on endlessly through the floods of conversation and champagne.

VI

The Romantic Movement

The French Revolution was like a bomb, to the making of which every liberal thinker and writer of the eighteenth century had lent a hand, and which, when it exploded, destroyed its creators. After the smoke had rolled away, it became clear that the old régime, with its despotisms and its persecutions, had indeed been abolished for ever; but the spirit of the *Philosophes* had vanished likewise. Men's minds underwent a great reaction. The traditions of the last two centuries were violently broken. In literature, particularly, it seemed as if the very foundations of the art must be laid anew; and, in this task, if men looked at all for inspiration from the Past, it was towards that age which differed most from the age of their fathers—towards those distant times before the Renaissance, when the medieval Church reigned supreme in Europe.

But before examining these new developments more closely, one glance must be given at a writer whose qualities had singularly little to do with his surroundings. ANDRÉ CHÉNIER passed the active years of his short life in the thick of the revolutionary ferment, and he was guillotined at the age of thirty-two; but his most characteristic poems might have been composed in some magic island, far from the haunts of men, and untouched by 'the rumour of periods'. He is the only French writer of the eighteenth century in whom the pure and undiluted spirit of poetry is manifest. For this reason, perhaps, he has often been acclaimed as the forerunner of the great Romantic outburst of a generation later; but, in reality, to give him such a title is to misjudge the whole value of his work. For he is essentially a classic; with a purity, a restraint, a measured and accomplished art which would have delighted Boileau, and which brings him into close kinship with Racine and La Fontaine. If his metrical technique is somewhat looser than the former poet's, it is infinitely less loose than the latter's; and his occasional departures from the strict classical canons of versification are always completely subordinated to the controlling balance of his style. In his *Églogues* the beauty of his workmanship often reaches perfection. The short poems are Attic in their serenity and their grace. It is not the rococo pseudo-classicism of the later versifiers of the eighteenth century, it is the delicate flavour of true Hellenism that breathes from them; and, as one reads them, one is reminded alternately of Theocritus and of Keats. Like Keats, Chénier was cut off when he had hardly more than given promise of what his achievement might have been. His brief and tragic apparition in the midst of the Revolution is like that of some lovely bird flitting on a sudden out of the darkness and the terror of a tempest, to be overcome a moment later, and whirled to destruction.

The lines upon which the Romantic Movement was to develop had no connexion whatever with Chénier's exquisite art. Throughout French Literature, it is easy to perceive two main impulses at work, which, between them, have inspired all the great masterpieces of the language. On the one hand, there is that positive spirit of searching and unmitigated common sense which has given French prose its peculiar distinction, which lies at the root of the wonderful critical powers of the nation, and which has produced that remarkable and persistent strain of Realism—of absolute fidelity to the naked truth—common to the earliest *Fabliaux* of the Middle Ages and the latest Parisian novel of to-day. On the other hand, there is in French literature a totally different—almost a contradictory—tendency, which is no less clearly marked and hardly less important—the tendency towards pure Rhetoric. This love of language for its own sake—of language artfully ordered, splendidly adorned, moving, swelling, irresistible—may be seen alike in the torrential sentences of Rabelais, in the sonorous periods of Bossuet, and in the passionate *tirades* of Corneille. With the great masters of the seventeenth century—Pascal, Racine, La Fontaine, La Bruyère—the two influences met, and achieved a perfect balance. In their work, the most penetrating realism is beautified and ennobled by all the resources of linguistic art, while the rhetorical instinct is preserved from pomposity and inflation by a supreme critical sense. With the eighteenth century, however, a change came. The age was a critical age— an age of prose and common sense; the rhetorical impulse faded away, to find expression only in melodramatic tragedy and dull verse; and the style of Voltaire, so brilliant and yet so colourless, so limited and yet so infinitely sensible, symbolized the literary character of the century. The Romantic Movement was an immense reaction against the realism which had come to such perfection in the acid prose of Voltaire. It was a reassertion of the rhetorical instinct in all its strength and in all its forms. There was no attempt simply to redress the balance; no wish to revive the studied perfection of the classical age. The realistic spirit was almost completely abandoned. The pendulum swung violently from one extreme to the other.

The new movement had been already faintly discernible in Diderot's bright colouring and the oratorical structure of Rousseau's writing. But it was not until after the Revolution, in the first years of the nineteenth century, that the Romantic spirit completely declared itself—in the prose of CHATEAUBRIAND. Chateaubriand was, at bottom, a rhetorician pure and simple—a rhetorician in the widest sense of the word. It was not merely that the resources of his style were enormous in colour, movement, and imagery, in splendour of rhythm, in descriptive force; but that his whole cast of mind was in itself rhetorical, and that he saw, felt, and thought with the same emphasis, the same amplitude, the same romantic sensibility with which he wrote. The three subjects which formed the main themes of all his work and gave occasion for his finest passages were Christianity, Nature, and himself. His conception of Christianity was the very reverse of that of the eighteenth century. In his *Génie du Christianisme* and his *Martyrs* the analytical and critical spirit of his predecessors has entirely vanished; the religion which they saw simply as a collection of theological dogmas, he envisioned as a living creed, arrayed in all the hues of poetry and imagination, and redolent with the mystery of the past. Yet it may be doubted whether Chateaubriand was essentially more religious than Voltaire. What Voltaire dissected in the dry light of reason, Chateaubriand invested with the cloak of his own eloquence—put it up, so to speak, on a platform, in a fine attitude, under a tinted illumination. He lacked the subtle intimacy of Faith. In his descriptions of Nature, too, the same characteristics appear. Compared with Rousseau's, they are far bolder, far richer, composed on a more elaborate and imposing scale; but they are less convincing; while Rousseau's landscapes are often profoundly moving, Chateaubriand's are hardly ever more than splendidly picturesque. There is a similar relation between the egoisms of the two men. Chateaubriand was never tired of writing about himself; and in his long *Mémoires d'Outre-Tombe*—the most permanently interesting of his works—he gave a full rein to his favourite passion. His conception of himself was Byronic. He swells forth, in all his pages, a noble, melancholy, proud, sentimental creature whom every man must secretly envy and every woman passionately adore. He had all the vanity of Rousseau, but none of his honesty. Rousseau, at any rate, never imposed upon himself; and Chateaubriand always did. Thus the vision that we have of him is of something wonderful but empty, something striking but unreal. It is the rhetorician that we see, and not the man.

Chateaubriand's influence was very great. Beside his high-flowing, romantic, imaginative writings, the tradition of the eighteenth century seemed to shrivel up into something thin, cold and insignificant. A new and dazzling world swam into the ken of his readers—a world in which the individual reigned in glory amid the glowing panorama of Nature and among the wondrous visions of a remote and holy past. His works became at once highly popular, though it was not until a generation later that their full effect was felt. Meanwhile, the impetus which he had started was continued in the poems of LAMARTINE. Here there is the same love of Nature, the same religious outlook, the same insistence on the individual point of view; but the tints are less brilliant, the emphasis is more restrained; the rhetorical impulse still dominates, but it is the rhetoric of elegiac tenderness rather than of picturesque pomp. A wonderful limpidity of versification which, while it is always perfectly easy, is never weak, and a charming quietude of sentiment which, however near it may seem to come to the commonplace, always just escapes it—these qualities give Lamartine a distinguished place in the literature of France. They may be seen in their perfection in the most famous of his poems, *Le Lac*, a monody descriptive of his feelings on returning alone to the shores of the lake where he had formerly passed the day with his mistress. And throughout all his poetical work precisely the same characteristics are to be found. Lamartine's lyre gave forth an inexhaustible flow of melody—always faultless, always pellucid, and always, in the same key.

DURING THE REVOLUTION, UNDER THE rule of Napoleon, and in the years which followed his fall, the energies of the nation were engrossed by war and politics. During these forty years there are fewer great names in French literature than in any other corresponding period since the Renaissance. At last, however, about the year 1830, a new generation of writers arose who brought back all the old glories and triumphantly proved that the French tongue, so far from having exhausted its resources, was a fresh and living instrument of extraordinary power. These writers—as has so often been the case in France—were bound together by a common literary creed. Young, ardent, scornful of the past, dazzled by the possibilities of the future, they raised the standard of revolt against the traditions of Classicism, promulgated a new aesthetic doctrine, and, after a sharp struggle and great excitement, finally succeeded in completely establishing their view. The change which they introduced was of enormous importance, and for this reason the date 1830 is a cardinal one in the literature of France. Every sentence, every verse that has been written in French since then bears upon it, somewhere or other, the imprint of the great Romantic Movement which came to a head in that year. What it was that was then effected—what the main differences are between French literature before 1830 and French literature after—deserves some further consideration.

The Romantic School—of which the most important members were VICTOR HUGO, ALFRED DE VIGNY, THÉOPHILE GAUTIER, ALEXANDRE DUMAS, and ALFRED DE MUSSET—was, as we have said, inspired by that supremely French love of Rhetoric which, during the long reign of intellect and prose in the eighteenth century, had been almost entirely suppressed. The new spirit had animated the prose of Chateaubriand and the poetry of Lamartine; but it was the spirit only: the *form* of both those writers retained most of the important characteristics of the old tradition. It was new wine in old bottles. The great achievement of the Romantic School was the creation of new bottles—of a new conception of form, in which the vast rhetorical impulse within them might find a suitable expression. Their actual innovations, however, were by no means sweeping. For instance, the numberless minute hard-and-fast metrical rules which, since the days of Malherbe, had held French poetry in shackles, they only interfered with to a very limited extent. They introduced a certain number of new metres; they varied the rhythm of the Alexandrine; but a great mass of petty and meaningless restrictions remained untouched, and no real attempt was made to get rid of them until more than a generation had passed. Yet here, as elsewhere, what they had done was of the highest importance. They had touched the ark of the covenant and they had not been destroyed. They had shown that it was possible to break a 'rule' and yet write good poetry. This explains the extraordinary violence of the Romantic controversy over questions of the smallest detail. When Victor Hugo, in the opening lines of *Hernani*, ventured to refer to an 'escalier dérobé', and to put 'escalier' at the end of one line, and 'dérobé' at the beginning of the next, he was assailed with the kind of virulence which is usually reserved for the vilest of criminals. And the abuse had a meaning in it: it was abuse of a revolutionary. For in truth, by the disposition of those two words, Victor Hugo had inaugurated a revolution. The whole theory of 'rules' in literature—the whole conception that there were certain definite traditional forms in existence which were, absolutely and inevitably, the best—was shattered for ever. The new doctrine was triumphantly vindicated—that the form of expression must depend ultimately, not upon tradition nor yet upon *a priori* reasonings, but simply and solely on the thing expressed.

The most startling and the most complete of the Romantic innovations related to the poetic Vocabulary. The number of words considered permissible in French poetry had been steadily diminishing since the days of Racine. A distinction had grown up between words that were 'noble' and words that were 'bas'; and only those in the former class were admitted into poetry. No word could be 'noble' if it was one ordinarily used by common people, or if it was a technical term, or if, in short, it was peculiarly expressive; for any such word would inevitably produce a shock, introduce mean associations, and destroy the unity of the verse. If the sense demanded the use of such a word, a periphrasis of 'noble' words must be employed instead. Racine had not been afraid to use the word 'chien' in the most exalted of his tragedies; but his degenerate successors quailed before such an audacity. If you must refer to such a creature as a dog, you had better call it 'de la fidélité respectable soutien'; the phrase actually occurs in a tragedy of the eighteenth century. It is clear that, with such a convention to struggle against, no poetry could survive. Everything bold, everything vigorous, everything surprising became an impossibility with a diction limited to the vaguest, most general, and most feebly pompous terms. The Romantics, in the face of violent opposition, threw the doors of poetry wide open to every word in the language. How great the change was, and what was the nature of the public opinion against which the Romantics had to fight, may be judged from the fact that the use of the word 'mouchoir' during a performance of *Othello* a few years before 1830 produced a riot in the theatre. To such a condition of narrowness and futility had the great Classical tradition sunk at last!

The enormous influx of words into the literary vocabulary which the Romantic Movement brought about had two important effects. In the first place, the range of poetical expression was infinitely increased. French literature came out of a little, ceremonious, antiquated drawing-room into the open air. With the flood of new words, a thousand influences which had never been felt before came into operation. Strangeness, contrast, complication, immensity, curiosity, grotesqueness, fantasy—effects of this kind now for the first time became possible and common in verse. But, one point must be noticed. The abolition of the distinction between words that were 'bas' and 'noble' did not at first lead (as might have been expected) to an increase of realism. Rather the opposite took place. The Romantics loved the new words not because they made easier the expression of actual facts, but for their power of suggestion, for the effects of remoteness, contrast, and multiplicity which could be produced by them—in fact, for their rhetorical force. The new vocabulary came into existence as an engine of rhetoric, not as an engine of truth. Nevertheless—and this was the second effect of its introduction—in the long run the realistic impulse in French literature was also immensely strengthened. The vocabulary of prose widened at the same time as that of verse; and the prose of the first Romantics remained almost completely rhetorical. But the realistic elements always latent in prose—and especially in French prose—soon asserted themselves; the vast opportunities for realistic description which the enlarged vocabulary opened out were eagerly seized upon; and it was not long before there arose in French literature a far more elaborate and searching realism than it had ever known before.

It was, perhaps, unfortunate that the main struggle of the Romantic controversy should have been centred in the theatre. The fact that this was so is an instance of the singular interest in purely literary questions which has so often been displayed by popular opinion in France. The controversy was not simply an academic matter for connoisseurs and critics to decide upon in private; it was fought out in all the heat of popular excitement on the public stage. But the wild enthusiasm aroused by the triumphs of Dumas and Hugo in the theatre shows, in a no less striking light, the incapacity of contemporaries to gauge the true significance of new tendencies in art. On the whole, the dramatic achievement of the Romantic School was the least valuable part of their work. *Hernani*, the first performance of which marked the turning-point of the movement, is a piece of bombastic melodrama, full of the stagiest clap-trap and the most turgid declamation. Victor Hugo imagined when he wrote it that he was inspired by Shakespeare; if he was inspired by anyone it was by Voltaire. His drama is the old drama of the eighteenth century, repainted in picturesque colours; it resembles those grotesque country-houses that our forefathers were so fond of, where the sham-Gothic turrets and castellations ill conceal the stucco and the pilasters of a former age. Of true character and true passion it has no trace. The action, the incidents, the persons—all alike are dominated by considerations of rhetoric, and of rhetoric alone. The rhetoric has, indeed, this advantage over that of *Zaïre* and *Alzire*—it is bolder and more highly coloured; but then it is also more pretentious. All the worst tendencies of the Romantic Movement may be seen completely displayed in the dramas of Victor Hugo.

For throughout his work that wonderful writer expressed in their extreme forms the qualities and the defects of his school. Above all, he was the supreme lord of words. In sheer facility, in sheer abundance of language, Shakespeare alone of all the writers of the world can be reckoned his superior. The bulk of his work is very great, and the nature of it is very various; but every page bears the mark of the same tireless fecundity, the same absolute dominion over the resources of speech. Words flowed from Victor Hugo like light from the sun. Nor was his volubility a mere disordered mass of verbiage: it was controlled, adorned, and inspired by an immense technical power. When one has come under the spell of that great enchanter, one begins to believe that his art is without limits, that with such an instrument and such a science there is no miracle which he cannot perform. He can conjure up the strangest visions of fancy; he can evoke the glamour and the mystery of the past; he can sing with exquisite lightness of the fugitive beauties of Nature; he can pour out, in tenderness or in passion, the melodies of love; he can fill his lines with the fire, the stress, the culminating fury, of prophetic denunciation; he can utter the sad and secret questionings of the human spirit, and give voice to the solemnity of Fate. In the long roll and vast swell of his verse there is something of the ocean—a moving profundity of power. His sonorous music, with its absolute sureness of purpose, and its contrapuntal art, recalls the vision in *Paradise Lost* of him who—

> *with volant touch*
> *Fled and pursued transverse the resonant fugue.*

What kind of mind, what kind of spirit, must that have been, one asks in amazement, which could animate with such a marvellous perfection the enormous organ of that voice?

But perhaps it would be best to leave the question unasked—or at least unanswered. For the more one searches, the clearer it becomes that the intellectual scope and the spiritual quality of Victor Hugo were very far from being equal to his gifts of expression and imagination. He had the powers of a great genius and the soul of an ordinary man. But that was not all. There have been writers of the highest excellence—Saint-Simon was one of them—the value of whose productions have been unaffected, or indeed even increased, by their personal inferiority. They could not have written better, one feels, if they had been ten times as noble and twenty times as wise as they actually were. But unfortunately this is not so with Victor Hugo. His faults—his intellectual weakness, his commonplace outlook, his lack of humour, his vanity, his defective taste—cannot be dismissed as irrelevant and unimportant, for they are indissolubly bound up with the very substance of his work. It was not as a mere technician that he wished to be judged; he wrote with a very different intention; it was as a philosopher, as a moralist, as a prophet, as a sublime thinker, as a profound historian, as a sensitive and refined human being. With a poet of such pretensions it is clearly most relevant to inquire whether his poetry does, in fact, reveal the high qualities he lays claim to, or whether, on the contrary, it is characterized by a windy inflation of sentiment, a showy superficiality of thought, and a ridiculous and petty egoism. These are the unhappy questions which beset the mature and reflective reader of Victor Hugo's works. To the young and enthusiastic one the case is different. For him it is easy to forget—or even not to observe—what there may be in that imposing figure that is unsatisfactory and second-rate. *He* may revel at will in the voluminous harmonies of that resounding voice; by turns thrilling with indignation, dreaming in ecstasy, plunging into abysses, and soaring upon unimaginable heights. Between youth and age who shall judge? Who decide between rapture and reflection, enthusiasm and analysis? To determine the precise place of Victor Hugo in the hierarchy of poets would be difficult indeed. But this much is certain: that at times the splendid utterance does indeed grow transfused with a pure and inward beauty, when the human frailties vanish, and all is subdued and glorified by the high purposes of art. Such passages are to be found among the lyrics of *Les Feuilles d'Automne, Les Rayons et Les Ombres, Les Contemplations*, in the brilliant descriptions and lofty imagery of *La Légende des Siècles*, in the burning invective of

Les Châtiments. None but a place among the most illustrious could be given to the creator of such a stupendous piece of word-painting as the description of the plain of Waterloo in the latter volume, or of such a lovely vision as that in *La Légende des Siècles*, of Ruth looking up in silence at the starry heaven. If only the wondrous voice had always spoken so!

THE ROMANTIC LOVE OF VASTNESS, richness, and sublimity, and the romantic absorption in the individual—these two qualities appear in their extremes throughout the work of Hugo: in that of ALFRED DE VIGNY it is the first that dominates; in that of ALFRED DE MUSSET, the second. Vigny wrote sparingly—one or two plays, a few prose works, and a small volume of poems; but he produced some masterpieces. A far more sober artist than Hugo, he was also a far profounder thinker, and a sincerer man. His melancholy, his pessimism, were the outcome of no Byronic attitudinizing, but the genuine intimate feelings of a noble spirit; and he could express them in splendid verse. His melancholy was touched with grandeur, his pessimism with sublimity. In his *Moïse*, his *Colère de Samson*, his *Maison du Berger*, his *Mont des Oliviers*, and others of his short reflective poems, he envisions man face to face with indifferent Nature, with hostile Destiny, with poisoned Love, and the lesson he draws is the lesson of proud resignation. In *La Mort du Loup*, the tragic spectacle of the old wolf driven to bay and killed by the hunters inspires perhaps his loftiest verses, with the closing application to humanity—'Souffre et meurs sans parler'—summing up his sad philosophy. No less striking and beautiful are the few short stories in his *Servitude et Grandeur Militaires*, in which some heroic incidents of military life are related in a prose of remarkable strength and purity. In the best work of Vigny there are no signs of the strain, the over-emphasis, the tendency towards the grotesque, always latent in Romanticism; its nobler elements are alone preserved; he has achieved the grand style.

Alfred de Musset presents a complete contrast. He was the spoilt child of the age—frivolous, amorous, sensuous, charming, unfortunate, and unhappy; and his poetry is the record of his personal feelings, his varying moods, his fugitive loves, his sentimental despairs.

> *Le seul bien qui me reste au monde*
> *Est d'avoir quelquefois pleuré,*

he exclaims, with an accent of regretful softness different indeed from that of Vigny. Among much that is feeble, ill constructed, and exaggerated in his verse, strains of real beauty and real pathos constantly recur. Some of his lyrics are perfect; the famous song of Fortunio in itself entitles him to a high place among the masters of the language; and in his longer pieces—especially in the four *Nuits*—his emotion occasionally rises, grows transfigured, and vibrates with a strange intensity, a long, poignant, haunting note. But doubtless his chief claim to immortality rests upon his exquisite little dramas (both in verse and prose), in which the romance of Shakespeare and the fantasy of Marivaux mingle with a wit, a charm, an elegance, which are all Musset's own. In his historical drama, *Lorenzaccio*, he attempted to fill a larger canvas, and he succeeded. Unlike the majority of the Romantics, Musset had a fine sense of psychology and a penetrating historical vision. In this brilliant, vivacious, and yet subtle tragedy he is truly great.

We must now glance at the effects which the Romantic Movement produced upon the art which was destined to fill so great a place in the literature of the nineteenth century—the art of prose fiction. With the triumph of Classicism in the seventeenth century, the novel, like all other forms of literature, grew simplified and compressed. The huge romances of Mademoiselle de Scudéry were succeeded by the delicate little stories of Madame de Lafayette, one of which—*La Princesse de Clèves*—a masterpiece of charming psychology and exquisite art, deserves to be considered as the earliest example of the modern novel. All through the eighteenth century the same tendency is visible. *Manon Lescaut*, the passionate and beautiful romance of l'Abbé Prévost, is a very small book, concerned, like *La Princesse de Clèves*, with two characters only— the lovers, whose varying fortunes make up the whole action of the tale. Precisely the same description applies to the subtle and brilliant *Adolphe* of Benjamin Constant, produced in the early years of the nineteenth century. Even when the framework was larger—as in Le Sage's *Gil Blas* and Marivaux's *Vie de Marianne*—the spirit was the same; it was the spirit of selection, of simplification, of delicate skill. Both the latter works are written in a prose style of deliberate elegance, and both consist rather of a succession of small incidents—almost of independent short stories—than of one large developing whole. The culminating example of the eighteenth-century form of fiction may be seen in the *Liaisons Dangereuses* of Laclos, a witty, scandalous and remarkably able novel, concerned with the interacting intrigues of a small society of persons, and revealing on every page a most brilliant and concentrated art. Far more modern, both in its general conception and in the absolute realism of its treatment, was Diderot's *La Religieuse*; but this masterpiece was not published till some years after the Revolution; and the real honour of having originated the later developments in French fiction—as in so many other branches of literature—belongs undoubtedly to Rousseau. *La Nouvelle Héloïse*, faulty as it is as a work of art, with its feeble psychology and loose construction, yet had the great merit of throwing open whole new worlds for the exploration of the novelist—the world of nature on the one hand, and on the other the world of social problems and all the living forces of actual life. The difference between the novels of Rousseau and those of Hugo is great; but yet it is a difference merely of degree. *Les Misérables* is the consummation of the romantic conception of fiction which Rousseau had adumbrated half a century before. In that enormous work, Hugo attempted to construct a prose epic of modern life; but the attempt was not successful. Its rhetorical cast of style, its ceaseless and glaring melodrama, its childish presentments of human character, its endless digressions and—running through all this—its evidences of immense and disordered power, make the book perhaps the most magnificent failure—the most 'wild enormity' ever produced by a man of genius. Another development of the romantic spirit appeared at about the same time in the early novels of George Sand, in which the ardours of passionate love are ecstatically idealized in a loose and lyric flow of innumerable words.

There can be little doubt that if the development of fiction had stopped at this point the infusion into it of the romantic spirit could only have been judged a disaster. From the point of view of art, such novels as those of Victor Hugo and the early works of George Sand were a retrogression from those of the eighteenth century. *Manon Lescaut*, tiny, limited, unambitious as it is, stands on a far higher level of artistic achievement than the unreal and incoherent *Les Misérables*. The scale of the novel had indeed been infinitely enlarged, but the apparatus for dealing adequately with the vast masses of new material was wanting. It is pathetic to watch the romantic novelists trying to infuse beauty and significance into their subjects by means of fine writing, lyrical outbursts, impassioned philosophical dissertations, and all the familiar rhetorical devices so dear to them. The inevitable result was something lifeless, formless, fantastic; they were on the wrong track. The true method for the treatment of their material was not that of rhetoric at all; it was that of realism. This fact was discovered by STENDHAL, who was the first to combine an enlarged view of the world with a plain style and an accurate, unimpassioned, detailed examination of actual life. In his remarkable novel, *Le Rouge et Le Noir*, and in some parts of his later work, *La Chartreuse de Parme*, Stendhal laid down the lines on which French fiction has been developing ever since. The qualities which distinguish him are those which have distinguished all the greatest of his successors—a subtle psychological insight, an elaborate attention to detail, and a remorseless fidelity to the truth.

Important as Stendhal is in the history of modern French fiction, he is dwarfed by the colossal figure of BALZAC. By virtue of his enormous powers, and the immense quantity and variety of his output, Balzac might be called the Hugo of prose, if it were not that in two most important respects he presents a complete contrast to his great contemporary. In the first place, his control of the technical resources of the language was as feeble as Hugo's was mighty. Balzac's style is bad; in spite of the electric vigour that runs through his writing, it is formless, clumsy, and quite without distinction; it is the writing of a man who was highly perspicacious, formidably powerful, and vulgar. But, on the other hand, he possessed one great quality which Hugo altogether lacked—the sense of the real. Hugo was most himself when he was soaring on the wings of fancy through the empyrean; Balzac was most himself when he was rattling in a hired cab through the streets of Paris. He was of the earth earthy. His coarse, large, germinating spirit gave forth, like the earth, a teeming richness, a solid, palpable creation. And thus it was he who achieved what Hugo, in *Les Misérables*, had in vain attempted. *La Comédie Humaine*, as he called the long series of his novels, which forms in effect a single work, presents, in spite of its limitations and its faults, a picture of the France of that age drawn on the vast scale and in the grand manner of an epic.

The limitations and the faults of Balzac's work are, indeed, sufficiently obvious and sufficiently grave. The same coarseness of fibre which appears in his style made him incapable of understanding the delicacies of life—the refined shades of emotion, the subtleties of human intercourse. He probably never read Jane Austen; but if he had he certainly would have considered her an utterly pointless writer; and he would have been altogether at sea in a novel by Henry James. The elusive things that are so important, the indecisive things that are so curious, the intimate things that are so thrilling—all these slipped through his rough, matter-of-fact grasp. His treatment of the relations between the sexes is characteristic. The subject fills a great place in his novels; he approaches it with an unflinching boldness, and a most penetrating gaze; yet he never succeeds in giving a really satisfactory presentment of the highest of those relations—love. That eluded him: its essence was too subtle, too private, too transcendental. No one can describe love who has not the makings of a poet in him. And a poet was the very last thing that Balzac was.

But his work does not merely suffer from the absence of certain good qualities; it is also marred by the presence of positively bad ones. Balzac was not simply a realist. There was a romantic vein in him, which occasionally came to the surface with unfortunate results. When that happened, he plunged into the most reckless melodrama, revelled in the sickliest sentiment, or evolved the most grotesque characters, the most fantastic plots. And these lapses occur quite indiscriminately. Side by side with some detailed and convincing description, one comes upon glaring absurdities; in the middle of some narrative of extraordinary actuality, one finds oneself among hissing villains, disguises, poisons, and all the paraphernalia of a penny novelette. Balzac's lack of critical insight into his own work is one of the most singular of his characteristics. He hardly seems to have known at all what he was about. He wrote feverishly, desperately, under the impulsion of irresistible genius. His conceptions crowded upon him in vivid, serried multitudes—the wildest visions of fantasy mixed pell-mell with the most vital realizations of fact. It was not for him to distinguish; his concern was simply, somehow or other, to get them all out: good, bad, or indifferent, what did it matter? The things were in his brain; and they must be expressed.

Fortunately, it is very easy for the reader to be more discriminating than Balzac. The alloy is not inextricably mingled with the pure metal—the chaff may be winnowed off, and the grain left. His errors and futilities cannot obscure his true achievement—his evocation of multitudinous life. The whole of France is crammed into his pages, and electrified there into intense vitality. The realism of the classical novelists was a purely psychological realism; it was concerned with the delicately shifting states of mind of a few chosen persons, and with nothing else. Balzac worked on a very different plan. He neglected the subtleties of the spirit, and devoted himself instead to, displaying the immense interest that lay in those prosaic circumstances of existence which the older writers had ignored. He showed with wonderful force that the mere common details of everyday life were filled with drama, that, to him who had eyes to see, there might be significance in a ready-made suit of clothes, and passion in the furniture of a boarding-house. Money in particular gave him an unending theme. There is hardly a character in the whole vast range of his creation of whose income we are not exactly informed; and it might almost be said that the only definite moral that can be drawn from *La Comédie Humaine* is that the importance of money can never be over-estimated. The classical writers preferred to leave such matters to the imagination of the reader; it was Balzac's great object to leave nothing to the imagination of the reader. By ceaseless effort, by infinite care, by elaborate attention to the minutest details, he would describe *all*. He brought an encyclopaedic knowledge to bear upon his task; he can give an exact account of the machinery of a provincial printing-press; he can write a dissertation on the methods of military organization; he can reveal the secret springs in the mechanism of Paris journalism; he is absolutely at home in the fraudulent transactions of money-makers, the methods of usurers, the operations of high finance. And into all this mass of details he can infuse the spirit of life. Perhaps his masterpiece in realistic description is his account of La Maison Vauquer—a low boarding-house, to which he devotes page after page of minute particularity. The result is not a mere dead catalogue: it is a palpitating image of lurid truth. Never was the sordid horror which lurks in places and in things evoked with a more intense completeness.

Undoubtedly it is in descriptions of the sordid, the squalid, the ugly, and the mean that Balzac particularly excels. He is at his greatest when he is revealing the horrible underside of civilization—the indignities of poverty, the low intrigues of parasites, the long procession of petty agonies that embitter and ruin a life. Over this world of shadow and grime he throws strange lights. Extraordinary silhouettes flash out and vanish; one has glimpses of obscure and ominous movements on every side; and, amid all this, some sudden vision emerges from the darkness, of pathos, of tenderness, of tragic and unutterable pain.

Balzac died in 1850, and at about that time the Romantic Movement came to an end. Victor Hugo, it is true, continued to live and to produce for more than thirty years longer; but French literature ceased to be dominated by the ideals of the Romantic school. That school had accomplished much; it had recreated French poetry, and it had revolutionized French prose. But, by the very nature of its achievement, it led the way to its own supersession. The spirit which animated its doctrines was the spirit of progress and of change; it taught that there were no fixed rules for writing well; that art, no less than science, lived by experiment; that a literature which did not develop was dead. Therefore it was inevitable that the Romantic ideal itself should form the stepping-stone for a fresh advance. The complex work of Balzac unites in a curious way many of the most important elements of the old school and of the new. Alike by his vast force, his immense variety, his formlessness, his lack of critical and intellectual power, he was a Romantic; but he belonged to the future in his enormous love of prosaic detail, his materialist cast of mind, and his preoccupation with actual facts.

VII

The Age of Criticism

With the generation of writers who rose to eminence after the death of Balzac, we come within the reach of living memory, so that a just estimate of their work is well-nigh impossible: it is so close to us that it is bound to be out of focus. And there is an additional difficulty in the extreme richness and variety of their accomplishment. They explored so many fields of literature, and produced so much of interest and importance, that a short account of their work can hardly fail to give a false impression of it. Only its leading characteristics and its most remarkable manifestations can be touched upon here.

The age was before all else an age of Criticism. A strong reaction set in against the looseness of construction and the extravagance of thought which had pervaded the work of the Romantics; and a new ideal was set up—an ideal which was to combine the width and diversity of the latter with the precision of form and the deliberate artistic purpose of the Classical age. The movement affected the whole of French literature, but its most important results were in the domain of Prose. Nowhere were the defects of the Romantics more obvious than in their treatment of history. With a very few exceptions they conceived of the past as a picturesque pageant—a thing of contrasts and costumes, an excuse for rhetorical descriptions, without inner significance or a real life of its own. One historian of genius they did indeed produce—MICHELET; and the contrast between his work and that of his successors, TAINE and RENAN, is typical of the new departure. The great history of Michelet, with its strange, convulsive style, its capricious and imaginative treatment of facts, and its undisguised bias, shows us the spectacle of the past in a series of lurid lightning-flashes—a spectacle at once intensely vivid and singularly contorted; it is the history of a poet rather than of a man of science. With Taine and Renan the personal element which forms the very foundation of Michelet's work has been carefully suppressed. It is replaced by an elaborate examination of detail, a careful, sober, unprejudiced reconstruction of past conditions, an infinitely conscientious endeavour to tell the truth and nothing but the truth. Nor is their history merely the dead bones of analysis and research; it is informed with an untiring sympathy; and—in the case of Renan especially—a suave and lucid style adds the charm and amenity which art alone can give.

The same tendencies appear to a still more remarkable degree in Criticism. With SAINTE-BEUVE, in fact, one might almost say that criticism, as we know it, came into existence for the first time. Before him, all criticism had been one of two things: it had been either a merely personal expression of opinion, or else an attempt to establish universal literary canons and to judge of writers by the standards thus set up. Sainte-Beuve realized that such methods—the slap-dash pronouncements of a Johnson or the narrow generalizations of a Boileau—were in reality not critical at all. He saw that the critic's first duty was not to judge, but to understand; and with this object he set himself to explore all the facts which could throw light on the temperament, the outlook, the ideals of his author; he examined his biography, the society in which he lived, the influences of his age; and with the apparatus thus patiently formed he proceeded to act as the interpreter between the author and the public. His *Causeries du Lundi*—short critical papers originally contributed to a periodical magazine and subsequently published in a long series of volumes—together with his *Port Royal*—an elaborate account of the movements in letters and philosophy during the earlier years of Louis XIV's reign—contain a mass of material of unequalled value concerning the whole of French literature. His analytical and sympathetic mind is reflected in the quiet wit and easy charm of his writing. Undoubtedly the lover of French literature will find in Sainte-Beuve's *Lundis* at once the most useful and the most agreeable review of the subject in all its branches; and the more his knowledge increases, the more eagerly will he return for further guidance and illumination to those delightful books.

But the greatest prose-writer of the age devoted himself neither to history nor to criticism—though his works are impregnated with the spirit of both—but to Fiction. In his novels, FLAUBERT finally accomplished what Balzac had spasmodically begun—the separation of the art of fiction from the unreality, the exaggeration, and the rhetoric of the Romantic School. Before he began to write, the movement towards a greater restraint, a more deliberate art, had shown itself in a few short novels by GEORGE SAND—the first of the long and admirable series of her mature works—where, especially in such delicate masterpieces as *La Mare au Diable*, *La Petite Fadette*, and *François le Champi*, her earlier lyricism and incoherence were replaced by an idyllic sentiment strengthened and purified by an exquisite sense of truth. Flaubert's genius moved in a very different and a far wider orbit: but it was no less guided by the dictates of deliberate art. In his realism, his love of detail, and his penetrating observation of facts, Flaubert was the true heir of Balzac; while in the scrupulosity of his style and the patient, laborious, and sober treatment of his material he presented a complete contrast to his great predecessor. These latter qualities make Flaubert the pre-eminent representative of his age. The critical sense possessed him more absolutely and with more striking results than all the rest of his contemporaries. His watchfulness over his own work was almost infinite. There has never been a writer who took his art with such a passionate seriousness, who struggled so incessantly towards perfection, and who suffered so acutely from the difficulties, the disappointments, the desperate, furious efforts of an unremitting toil. His style alone cost him boundless labour. He would often spend an entire day over the elaboration and perfection of a single sentence, which, perhaps, would be altogether obliterated before the publication of the book. He worked in an apoplectic fervour over every detail of his craft—eliminating repetitions, balancing rhythms, discovering the precise word for every shade of meaning, with an extraordinary, an almost superhuman, persistence. And in the treatment of his matter his conscientiousness was equally great. He prepared for his historical novels by profound researches in the original authorities of the period, and by personal visits to the localities he intended to describe. When he treated of modern life he was no less scrupulously exact. One of his scenes was to pass in a cabbage-garden by moonlight. But what did a cabbage-garden by moonlight really look like? Flaubert waited long for a propitious night, and then went out, notebook in hand, to take down the precise details of what he saw. Thus it was that his books were written very slowly, and his production comparatively small. He spent six years over the first and most famous of his works—*Madame Bovary*; and he devoted no less than thirteen to his encyclopedic *Bouvard et Pécuchet*, which was still unfinished when he died.

The most abiding impression produced by the novels of Flaubert is that of solidity. This is particularly the case with his historical books. The bric-à-brac and fustian of the Romantics has disappeared, to be replaced by a clear, detailed, profound presentment of the life of the past. In *Salammbô*, ancient Carthage rises up before us, no crazy vision of a picturesque and disordered imagination, but in all the solidity of truth; coloured, not with the glaring contrasts of rhetoric, but with the real blaze of an eastern sun; strange, not with an imported fantastic strangeness manufactured in nineteenth-century Paris, but with the strangeness—so much more mysterious and significant—of the actual, barbaric Past.

The same characteristics appear in Flaubert's modern novels. *Madame Bovary* gives us a picture of life in a French provincial town in the middle of the last century—a picture which, with its unemphatic tones, its strong, sensitive, and accurate drawing, its masterly design, produces an effect of absolutely convincing veracity. The character and the fate of the wretched woman who forms the central figure of the story come upon us, amid the grim tepidity of their surroundings, with extraordinary force. Flaubert's genius does not act in sudden flashes, but by the method of gradual accumulation. The effects which it produces are not of the kind that overwhelm and astonish, but of the more subtle sort that creep into the mind by means of a thousand details, an infinitude of elaborated fibres, and which, once there, are there for ever.

The solidity of Flaubert's work, however, was not unaccompanied with drawbacks. His writing lacks fire; there is often a sense of effort in it; and, as one reads his careful, faultless, sculpturesque sentences, it is difficult not to long, at times, for some of the irregular vitality of Balzac. Singularly enough, Flaubert's correspondence—one of the most interesting collections of letters in the language—shows that, so far as his personal character was concerned, irregular vitality was precisely one of his dominating qualities. But in his fiction he suppressed this side of himself in the interests, as he believed, of art. It was his theory that a complete detachment was a necessary condition for all great writing; and he did his best to put this theory into practice. But there was one respect in which he did not succeed in his endeavour. His hatred and scorn of the mass of humanity, his conception of them as a stupid, ignorant, and vulgar herd, appears throughout his work, and in his unfinished *Bouvard et Pécuchet* reaches almost to the proportion of a monomania. The book is an infinitely elaborate and an infinitely bitter attack on the ordinary man. There is something tragic in the spectacle of this lonely, noble, and potent genius wearing out his life at last over such a task—in a mingled agony of unconscious frenzied self-expression and deliberate misguided self-immolation.

In poetry, the reaction against Romanticism had begun with the *Émaux et Camées* of THÉOPHILE GAUTIER—himself in his youth one of the leaders of the Romantic School; and it was carried further in the work of a group of writers known as the *Parnassiens*—the most important of whom were LECONTE DE LISLE, SULLY PRUDHOMME, and HEREDIA. Their poetry bears the same relation to that of Musset as the history of Renan bears to that of Michelet, and the prose of Flaubert to that of Hugo. It is restrained, impersonal, and polished to the highest degree. The bulk of it is not great; but not a line of it is weak or faulty; and it possesses a firm and plastic beauty, well expressed by the title of Gautier's volume, and the principles of which are at once explained and exemplified in his famous poem beginning—

> *Oui, l'oeuvre sort plus belle*
> *D'une forme au travail*
> *Rebelle,*
> *—Vers, marbre, onyx, émail.*

The *Parnassiens* particularly devoted themselves to classical subjects, and to descriptions of tropical scenes. Their rich, sonorous, splendidly-moulded language invests their visions with a noble fixity, an impressive force. Among the gorgeous descriptive pieces of Leconte de Lisle, the exquisite lyrics of Sully Prudhomme, and the chiselled sonnets of Heredia some of the finest and weightiest verse of the century is to be found.

The age produced one other poet who, however, by the spirit of his work, belongs rather to the succeeding epoch than to his own. This was BAUDELAIRE, whose small volume—*Les Fleurs du Mal*—gives him a unique place among the masters of the poetic art. In his form, indeed, he is closely related to his contemporaries. His writing has all the care, the balance, the conscientious polish of the *Parnassiens*; it is in his matter that he differs from them completely. He was not interested in classical imaginations and impersonal descriptions; he was concerned almost entirely with the modern life of Paris and the actual experiences of a disillusioned soul. As intensely personal as the *Parnassiens* were detached, he poured into his verse all the gloom of his own character, all the bitterness of his own philosophy, all the agony of his own despair. Some poets—such as Keats and Chénier—in spite of the misfortunes of their lives, seem to distil nothing but happiness and the purest beauty into their poetry; they only come to their true selves amid the sunlight and the flowers. Other writers—such as Swift and Tacitus— rule supreme over the kingdom of darkness and horror, and their finest pages are written in the Valley of the Shadow of Death. Writers of this kind are very rarely poets; and it is Baudelaire's great distinction that he was able to combine the hideous and devastating conceptions of complete pessimism with the passion, the imagination, and the formal beauty that only live in magnificent verse. He is the Swift of poetry. His vision is black and terrible. Some of his descriptions are even more disgusting than those of Swift, and most of his pages are no fit reading for the young and ignorant. But the wise reader will find in this lurid poetry elements of profundity and power which are rare indeed. Above all, he will find in it a quality not common in French poetry—a passionate imagination which clothes the thought with splendour, and lifts the strange words of this unhappy mortal into the deathless regions of the sublime.

Conclusion

With the death of Flaubert in 1880, French literature entered upon a new phase—a phase which, in its essential qualities, has lasted till to-day, and which forms a suitable point for the conclusion of the present sketch.

This last phase has been dominated by two men of genius. In prose, MAUPASSANT carried on the work of Flaubert with a sharper manner and more vivid style, though with a narrower range. He abandoned the exotic and the historical visions of his predecessor, and devoted himself entirely, in his brilliant novels and yet more brilliant short stories, to an almost fiendishly realistic treatment of modern life. A precisely contrary tendency marks the poetry of VERLAINE. While Maupassant completely disengaged prose from every alien element of poetry and imagination, pushing it as far as it could go in the direction of incisive realism, Verlaine and his fellow-workers in verse attempted to make poetry more truly poetical than it had ever been before, to introduce into it the vagueness and dreaminess of individual moods and spiritual fluctuations, to turn it away from definite fact and bring it near to music.

It was with Verlaine and his successors that French verse completely broke away from the control of those classical rules, the infallibility of which had been first attacked by the Romantics. In order to express the delicate, shifting, and indecisive feelings which he loved so well, Verlaine abolished the last shreds of rhythmical regularity, making his verse a perfectly fluid substance, which he could pour at will into the subtle mould of his feeling and his thought. The result justified the means. Verlaine's poetry exhales an exquisite perfume—strange, indistinct, and yet, after the manner of perfume, unforgettable. Listening to his enchanting, poignant music, we hear the trembling voice of a soul. This last sad singer carries us back across the ages, and, mingling his sweet strain with the distant melancholy of Villon, symbolizes for us at once the living flower and the unchanging root of the great literature of France.

WE HAVE NOW TRACED THE main outlines of that literature from its dim beginnings in the Dark Ages up to the threshold of the present time. Looking back over the long line of writers, the first impression that must strike us is one of extraordinary wealth. France, it is true, has given to the world no genius of the colossal stature and universal power of Shakespeare. But, then, where is the equal of Shakespeare to be found? Not even in the glorious literature of Greece herself. Putting out of account such an immeasurable magnitude, the number of writers of the first rank produced by France can be paralleled in only one other modern literature—that of England. The record is, indeed, a splendid one which contains, in poetry and drama, the names of Villon, Ronsard, Corneille, Molière, Racine, La Fontaine, Chénier, Lamartine, Hugo, Vigny, Gautier, Baudelaire, Verlaine; and in prose those of Froissart, Rabelais, Montaigne, Pascal, Bossuet, La Rochefoucauld, La Bruyère, Montesquieu, Saint-Simon, Voltaire, Diderot, Rousseau, Chateaubriand, Balzac, Flaubert, and Maupassant. And, besides this great richness and variety, another consideration gives a peculiar value to the literature of France. More than that of any other nation in Europe, it is distinctive and individual; if it had never existed, the literature of the world would have been bereft of certain qualities of the highest worth which France alone has been able to produce. Where else could we find the realism which would replace that of Stendhal and Balzac, Flaubert and Maupassant? Where else should we look for the brilliant lucidity and consummate point which Voltaire has given us? Or the force and the precision that glow in Pascal? Or the passionate purity that blazes in Racine?

Finally, if we would seek for the essential spirit of French literature, where shall we discover it? In its devotion to truth? In its love of rhetoric? In its clarity? In its generalizing power? All these qualities are peculiarly its own, but, beyond and above them, there is another which controls and animates the rest. The one high principle which, through so many generations, has guided like a star the writers of France is the principle of deliberation, of intention, of a conscious search for ordered beauty; an unwavering, an indomitable pursuit of the endless glories of art.

A Note About the Author

Lytton Strachey (1880–1932) was an English writer and critic, best known for his innovation in the biographical genre. After starting his career by writing reviews and critical articles for periodicals, Strachey reached his first great success and crowning achievement with the publication of *Eminent Victorians*, which defied the conventional standards of biographical work. Strachey was a founding member of the Bloomsburg Group, a club of English artists, writers, intellectuals and philosophers. Growing very close to some of the members, Strachey participated in an open three-way relationship with Dora Carrington, a painter, and Ralph Partridge. Stachey published a total of fourteen major works, eight of which were publish posthumously.

A Note from the Publisher

Spanning many genres, from non-fiction essays to literature classics to children's books and lyric poetry, Mint Edition books showcase the master works of our time in a modern new package. The text is freshly typeset, is clean and easy to read, and features a new note about the author in each volume. Many books also include exclusive new introductory material. Every book boasts a striking new cover, which makes it as appropriate for collecting as it is for gift giving. Mint Edition books are only printed when a reader orders them, so natural resources are not wasted. We're proud that our books are never manufactured in excess and exist only in the exact quantity they need to be read and enjoyed.

Discover more of your favorite classics with Bookfinity™.

- Track your reading with custom book lists.
- Get great book recommendations for your personalized Reader Type.
- Add reviews for your favorite books.
- AND MUCH MORE!

Visit **bookfinity.com** and take the fun Reader Type quiz to get started.

Enjoy our classic and modern companion pairings!

Printed in the USA
CPSIA information can be obtained
at www.ICGtesting.com
JSHW080000150824
68134JS00020B/2191

9 781513 278490